Empath:
An Empowering Book for the Highly Sensitive Person on How to Utilize Your Unique Ability and Maximize Your Human Potential

Positive Psychology Coaching Series

Copyright © 2017 by Ian Tuhovsky

Author's blog: www.mindfulnessforsuccess.com
Author's Amazon profile: amazon.com/author/iantuhovsky
Instagram profile: https://instagram.com/mindfulnessforsuccess

All rights reserved. No part of this publication may be reproduced, stored in a retrieval system, or transmitted, in any form or by any means, electronic, mechanical, photocopying, recording or otherwise without the prior written permission of the author and the publishers.

The scanning, uploading, and distribution of this book via the Internet, or via any other means, without the permission of the author is illegal and punishable by law.

Please purchase only authorized electronic editions, and do not participate in or encourage electronic piracy of copyrighted materials.

Important

The book is not intended to provide medical advice or to take the place of medical advice and treatment from your personal physician. Readers are advised to consult their own doctors or other qualified health professionals regarding the treatment of medical conditions. The author shall not be held liable or responsible for any misunderstanding or misuse of the information contained in this book. The information is not indeed to diagnose, treat or cure any disease.

It's important to remember that the author of this book is not a doctor/therapist/medical professional. Only opinions based upon his own personal experiences or research are cited. The author does not offer medical advice or prescribe any treatments. For any health or medical issues – you should be talking to your doctor first.

Please be aware that every e-book and "short read" I publish is written truly by me, with thoroughly researched content 100% of the time. Unfortunately, there's a huge number of low quality, cheaply outsourced spam titles on the Kindle non-fiction market these days, created by various internet marketing companies. **I don't tolerate these books. I want to provide you with high quality, so if you think that one of my books/short reads can be improved in any way, please contact me at:**

contact@mindfulnessforsuccess.com

I will be very happy to hear from you, because that's who I write my books for!

Introduction **4**
Chapter 1: What Is an Empath? **8**
Chapter 2: Am I an Empath? **12**
Chapter 3: The Science Behind Empathic Abilities **15**
Chapter 4: The Upside of Being an Empath **19**
Chapter 5: Challenges Empaths Face **23**
Chapter 6: Empaths & Health **27**
Chapter 7: Young Empaths **30**
Chapter 8: Empaths, The Workplace, & Career Choices **34**
Chapter 9: Empaths & Spirituality **37**
Chapter 10: Empaths & Emotional Intelligence **40**
Chapter 11: Why The World Needs Empaths **43**
Part II **47**
Chapter 12: Working with Your Emotions & Staying Balanced **48**
Chapter 13: The Importance of Setting Boundaries & Asserting Yourself **53**
Chapter 14: Detecting & Clearing Negative Energy **57**
Chapter 15: How to Handle Conflict As An Empath **61**
Chapter 16: How to Handle Energy Vampires **65**
Chapter 17: How to Handle a Toxic Romantic Relationship **70**
Chapter 18: Connecting with Other Empaths **74**
Chapter 19: Masculine, Feminine, or Both? **78**
Chapter 20: Letting Go & Coming to Terms With The Past **82**
Chapter 21: Staying in Harmony With Your Environment **86**
Chapter 22: Conclusion - How to Make The World A Better Place With Your Gift **90**
My Free Gift to You – Get One of My Audiobooks For Free! **93**
Recommended Reading for You **94**
About The Author **107**

Introduction

Have others ever told you to "stop being so sensitive"? Have you ever looked at other people and wondered how they manage to get through the day without noticing the suffering going on all around them? Do you feel so emotionally delicate in comparison to your peers that you have tried to block out what is going on around you? You may have even resorted to coping mechanisms such as overeating, overworking, or smoking as a means of managing your emotions. Maybe you have tried to "grow a thicker skin," or attempted to cover up your feelings with humor? Perhaps you have always felt different to others since childhood, but could never quite put your finger on why.

If this description resonates with you, congratulations! You may well be an empath. This puts you in the small group of people who not only understand the emotions of others, but literally feel them too. **In this book, you are going to discover exactly why you are so attuned to people in your environment, how to overcome common challenges the typical empath will face, and how to get the best from your gift.** You will understand why other people can leave you feeling energized one day, and drained the next. You will learn why you are more sensitive than the average person to illness and injury, and how to protect your well-being. Most important of all, you will discover exactly why you should avoid particular types of people and, if you have no choice but to live or work alongside them, how you can stop them dragging you down.

An empath who lacks insight into their own nature is likely to be miserable. If you have no idea why you are so readily affected by the emotions of others, you will become psychologically unstable. You will be unsure as to where your true feelings end, and those of other people begin. Hypersensitivity can be a burden if not properly managed, which is why it's so important that all empaths learn to harness the special gift they have been given. That's where this book comes in. Millions of other people around the world share your gifts and lead happy, fulfilling lives.

My reason for writing this book is simple. I am an empath who only came to terms with my talents a few years ago, and I want to help others along their journey. Although I had always been labeled "the sensitive one" as a child, and was prone to extreme mood swings as a teenager, it wasn't until my mid-twenties that I took a long, hard look at my personality. It all started when my life took an unexpected direction. In brief, I had a hellish six months. My relationship of six years ended, and one of my best friends died. None of my friends were surprised when I entered a state of deep depression. The pills prescribed to me by my physician didn't work, so with some reluctance I dragged myself to see a psychotherapist.

As it turned out, this was the smartest move I could have made. I started therapy with the intention of working through my depression but by the third session my therapist, Christie, started digging deeper into my past. We uncovered several recurring themes, one of which was my sensitivity to others. I confessed that other people's moods had always affected me, and that if they criticized me – even in a joking manner – then I would feel wounded for hours or sometimes days afterwards. To make matters worse, colleagues, friends and even relatives would roll their eyes or make passive-aggressive comments whenever I dared tell them how much they had hurt me.

During our fifth session, Christie raised the possibility that I might be an empath, or at least a "Highly Sensitive Person." At the time, I had no idea what she was talking about. Thankfully, I have always been a curious individual and so began researching the subject, connecting with other empaths, and learning how to make the most of my talents. I've come a long way. No longer am I overwhelmed by others' emotions, or feel like a freak for needing solitude and time away from even my closest friends. I have also been able to connect with other empaths via the internet. On one hand, it has been wonderful to talk with other empaths. At the same time, I found that many empaths struggle to understand their gift and even wish they could "turn it off." **I started to wonder how I could help these people and, in my own small way, encourage them to live up to their full potential.**

That's where this book comes in. It is written for empaths at all stages of their journey, from those who have yet to put a name to their condition, to those who are adept at handling the heavy emotions that are part and parcel of everyday life. Although our culture associates feelings and empathy with women, there are many male empaths out there. I hope that this book will help empaths of all genders. As most of us know, men living in Western cultures are not encouraged to talk about, or demonstrate, their vulnerable side. This is a real shame, as empathic men have plenty to offer the world. It took me a while to unpick the cultural conditioning that shaped my views of masculinity, but eventually I managed to accept that being a "real man" and "working with my emotions" were far from mutually exclusive. In my opinion, strong men (and women!) are willing to explore their feelings and embrace their empathic abilities. If you are a male empath, try to suspend everything you have been taught about men and emotions as you read and absorb the information in this book.

If you are a woman, then you will probably feel more comfortable talking about your experiences. At the same time, we still have a long way to go in supporting people to really open up about their innermost feelings. Female empaths also need guidance in coming to terms with their abilities in a culture that tends to look down on expressive individuals, labeling them as "silly," "melodramatic," or even "histrionic." It's no wonder that both empaths and non-empaths alike hesitate to talk about our emotional and mental health. Fortunately, things are slowly changing for the better. The medical community is starting to acknowledge that patients are not simply case studies to be solved, but multifaceted individuals with a range of psychological and emotional needs.

This book is also written for people who love and work with empaths. By taking the time to understand what it's like to be an empath, you will be in a position to offer your support when they inevitably feel overwhelmed by their own emotions and those of other people. Empaths make great friends, partners, relatives, and colleagues. However, they have a special set of needs. I know that had those closest to me read up on what it actually means to be an empath, I might have enjoyed better relationships.

This brings me to my final point. As a misunderstood bunch of people, many of us had difficult childhoods and have endured years of unsatisfying relationships, invalidation, confusion, and perhaps even abuse. If we are not careful, we can look back on the past and become mired in bitterness and regret. **My intention is to help empaths process what has already happened in their lives as they forge a new identity.** Later, I will teach you how to come to terms with your past, and look to the future with a sense of optimism.

The first part of this book will help you appreciate what it means to be an empath, and how this ability manifests in all areas of an individual's life. The second part contains practical tips for those looking to live a more productive, happier life whilst developing and maintaining their gift. Turn the page to begin learning exactly what the term "empath" really means.

Your Free Mindfulness E-book

I really appreciate the fact that you took an interest in my work!

I also think it's great you are into self-development and proactively making your life better.

This is why I would love to offer you a free, complimentary 120-page e-book.

It's about Mindfulness-Based Stress and Anxiety Management Techniques.

It will provide you with a solid foundation to kick-start your self-development success and help you become much more relaxed, and at the same time, a more focused and effective person. All explained in plain English, it's a useful free supplement to this book.

To download your e-book, please visit:

http://www.tinyurl.com/mindfulnessgift

Enjoy!
Thanks again for being my reader! It means a lot to me!

Chapter 1: What Is an Empath?

Most of us are familiar with the concept of empathy. Aside from sociopaths, who are largely incapable of appreciating what another individual may be feeling, humans are generally able to understand what others are going through in most situations. For example, suppose your friend tells you that her beloved father has died. Drawing on your own experiences of loss, you will instantly be able to appreciate that your friend will be feeling very sad. It's an automatic process that has helped us become so successful as a species. Empathy provides us with a means of bonding, which in turn cements our relationships. It wouldn't be very satisfying to spend time with someone who never had a clue what you were feeling, would it? That's why we tend to be drawn to those who accept our emotions, and who show signs that they truly understand what is happening to us.

An empath takes this common human ability to extremes. To be an empath is not merely to understand what someone feels on an intellectual level, but to experience it within your own mind and body. An empath can be talking to someone who feels depressed and, even if they are making a conscious effort to conceal their mental state, still be able to tune into this person's mood. They may suddenly feel tired, sad, or "heavy." **Empaths who have yet to learn about their own abilities are often confused by their own mood swings.** It can come as a relief to realize that they are not mad – just liable to feel the effects of other people's moods.[1]

You may have heard the term "Highly Sensitive Person" used in reference to empaths. The two concepts are closely related, but it is important to distinguish between them. "Highly Sensitive Person" (or Highly Sensitive People in plural form) is a term that applies to approximately 15-20% of the population. **Whilst all empaths are highly sensitive, not all sensitive people are empaths.** Dr. Elaine Aron, a leader in the field of HSP research, describes this kind of heightened sensitivity using the acronym D.O.E.S.

This is a useful starting point in understanding empathic abilities, as all empaths fit this criteria.[2]

The "D" stands for "Depth of processing," and refers to an individual's tendency

---

[1] Orloff, J. (2017). *The Empath's Survival Guide: Life Strategies for Sensitive People.* Sounds True: Boulder, Colorado.
[2] Aron, E. (2013). How Do You Recognize an HSP? hsperson.com

to think about the world in a measured yet creative manner. For example, a sensitive person or empath will take their time to think over various options available to them, but then put forward a well-reasoned case for whatever path they take. They are often good at long-term planning, as they can see how their actions today will influence future outcomes. They will usually be conscientious when it comes to work. The motto "Don't do today what you can put off until tomorrow" does not apply here!

"O" is for "Overstimulated." Highly sensitive people and empaths possess the ability to notice even subtle details and changes in the environment. Noticing and processing this much information is tiring. This is why sensitive people and empaths usually need plenty of time alone, particularly following a social event or trip to a busy place. Personally, I find the thought of attending a large party for more than a couple of hours to be very intimidating. Without even meaning to do so, I can't help but take in every little detail of my surroundings. There is no way of turning this ability off! If the music at a party is particularly noisy, I soon develop a headache.

Sensitive people and empaths are more emotionally reactive than others, hence the "E" in D.O.E.S. In other words, we feel things more deeply than other people. This applies in both positive and negative situations. Sometimes even a minor achievement such as lifting a slightly heavier weight at the gym makes me incredibly happy. At the same time, bad news affects me to a far greater extent than it does my partner and friends. When my friend died, I fell into a state of grief so deep that only therapy pulled me through. I thought I was abnormal, even weak, but I later discovered this kind of response is typical for an empath. The "E" also stands for "Empathy," refers to a sensitive person's greater-than-average ability to detect what someone else is feeling. However, a sensitive person is still within the "normal" range when it comes to picking up emotions in others. Remember that an empath's abilities in this area are much more well-developed.

Finally, the "S" stands for "Sensing the subtle." Sometimes this is referred to as "sensory processing sensitivity." Sensitive people and empaths are excellent at picking up on sensory information in the environment such as new scents, changes in temperature, and quiet background noises such as a ticking clock or water dripping from a roof. If you often find yourself saying "Can you hear that? That annoying noise?" or asking whether other people in the room would mind if you adjusted the temperature, this is a good sign that you possess sensory processing sensitivity. Some sensitive people and empaths have one or more particularly well-developed senses. In my case, it's the sense of smell. I can always tell when someone has changed their perfume or air freshener, and food smells make me feel physically sick if I am not hungry.

When I read the D.O.E.S. criteria for the first time, a lot of things fell into place. I was often praised for my good ideas in meetings, but sometimes urged to hurry up in completing projects. I often pointed out little details in the environment that others had missed, and I've had to leave social events on numerous occasions just because I felt so overwhelmed.

Empaths are highly sensitive people who not only show the traits listed above, but also have the capacity to feel other people's emotions. We don't yet know how what percentage of the general population are empaths. However, based on Dr. Aron's estimate that 15-20% of the population are highly sensitive people, and bearing in mind that only a minority of highly sensitive people are empaths, 5% is a reasonable guess. In summary, empaths are not common, but neither are they incredibly rare.

Dr. Judith Orloff, widely considered an expert in the field of empath studies, notes that there are two key categories of empathic abilities. The first category describes empathic responses to physical sensations. For example, if you are seated next to a colleague with visible eczema on their arm, your own skin will start to itch. If your child is sick, you will start feeling waves of nausea. The second category of empathic ability is the power to "take on" other people's emotions. For instance, an empath may be sat with two friends enjoying a delicious dinner, yet if one of their friends is feeling depressed, the empath will walk away feeling low. The stronger the emotion felt by the other person, the greater the effect they will have on the empath. This is inconvenient – to say the least – when that person is in a bad mood, or has a generally toxic personality.[3]

When I first started to research empaths in an attempt to make sense of my experiences, I realized that even a brief conversation with my next-door neighbor would leave me feeling tired for a couple of hours, even though she was a perfectly nice woman. After some thought, it hit me – whilst she was always polite, almost every word out of her mouth was a complaint or piece of criticism. Whether it was her most recent illness, the trouble she'd had with the bank that morning, or her sister's divorce, she would almost relish talking about it in detail. I nicknamed her "The Soulsucker." **Empaths are especially sensitive to this kind of person.**

---

[3] Orloff, J. (2017). *The Empath's Survival Guide: Life Strategies for Sensitive People.* Sounds True: Boulder, Colorado.

As you might expect of those who are prone to sensory overload, highly sensitive people and empaths are usually introverts. However, this is not always the case. Some are better able than others to cope with social situations, and are able to replenish their energy by spending time around other people. If you are an empath with a social circle filled with positive, upbeat individuals, then they can be a great source of emotional nourishment. At the same time, even positive emotions such as happiness and excitement can be too much for an empath or highly sensitive person to deal with. If this all sounds familiar, turn the page for further guidance as to how you can determine whether you are an empath.

Chapter 2: Am I an Empath?

There is no medical test you can take in order to determine whether you are an empath. However, a bit of introspection and self-analysis will help you arrive at the right conclusion. Thanks to the work of experts in the field such as Judith Orloff[4] and Elaine Aron[5], anyone can read a description of empaths and make an educated guess as to whether the term fits them. It may also help you to know that empathic abilities occur on a spectrum. Not all empaths are the same. Some are particularly sensitive to environmental factors such as bright lights and noise, whereas others are so in touch with the emotions of those around them that they avoid all events that require them to be in the same room as a big crowd.

First of all, consider whether you or others describe your intuition as "sharp" or "well-developed." Empaths quickly form strong opinions about people and situations. If you are an empath, you will have noticed that you can accurately judge someone's character within seconds of meeting them. You will also be able to detect whether someone is lying or has an ulterior motive. If you have ever spotted a liar well before anyone else, chances are that you are an empath.

Now think back to your childhood. Empaths are born with their gift, and therefore their abilities will manifest at a young age. You will probably be able to remember many instances whereby you demonstrated unusual sensitivity to other people's feelings and experiences. Your parents may have dismissed them as mere coincidence or luck, but over time a pattern will have emerged that continues to this day. As you moved into adolescence, you may have realized that you really were "different." **Teenage empaths are typically more mature than their peers, and prefer solitary activities rather than group activities and big parties.** You were probably a conscientious student, and praised by the adults around you for being so "good."

The next question relates to the labels family and friends use to describe you. Empaths are usually told that they are "sensitive," "in touch with the feelings of others," and "shy." Unfortunately, they may also be described as "haughty," "aloof," or "sullen." **This is because an overwhelmed empath quickly shuts down in stimulating situations, sometimes**

---
[4] Ibid.
[5] Aron, E. (1999). *The Highly Sensitive Person*. HarperCollins: London, England.

making them appear somewhat unfriendly. If you have often heard other people refer to you using any of the above words and phrases, there is a good chance that you are an empath. Some family members may even have teased or bullied you on the grounds that you are too sensitive.

Now think about your physical and mental health. Empaths will usually report physical and psychological disturbances following contact with anything with the power to provoke a strong emotional response. You may feel this on a psychological level, a physical level, or both. **For example, you may go out of your way to avoid conflict with others because arguments not only leave you feeling upset, but physically sick.** Spending time in a busy crowd may trigger a headache, because you are tuning into the mood states of many people at the same time. You are also more likely than other people to pick up colds and stomach bugs, to bruise more easily, and to show signs of allergy and intolerances. If you are an empath and suffer from ongoing physical symptoms such as fatigue, digestive disturbances or itchy skin, get tested for allergies. An intolerance to gluten, lactose or other allergens can have a serious negative impact on your overall well-being.

Empaths are generally more sensitive to caffeine and medications compared to their peers. You probably need a lower dose of medicine to feel the same effects as a non-empath. In addition, you are more likely to experience side-effects than the average patient. Your doctor might be quick to dismiss your concerns as being "all in your head," but they are real enough to you!

Your behavior and responses in intimate relationships provide another set of clues. Empaths enjoy being around their loved ones, and also feel inclined to help whenever those they care for encounter setbacks. **Yet they also tend to feel trapped or suffocated in romantic and sexual relationships.** This is frustrating for both the empath and their partner, because they will both wonder why the former can't seem to enjoy emotional and physical intimacy to the same extent as the latter. An empath's reluctance to get close to others isn't caused by a lack of love. It's simply because their partner's emotions are an ongoing source of stimulation that can prove overwhelming at times. If partners or close friends have often said that you appear withdrawn or emotionally unavailable, this is a reliable indicator that you are a highly sensitive person and possess empathic traits too.

Your response to art and music is another factor to consider. If you look at a particularly evocative painting, do you feel moved on a deep level? Whenever I go to an art gallery, I have to be careful not to stare too long at any portraits of people who look remotely upset or angry.

Even though they are merely paintings, I still feel the emotions depicted as though they are my own. If you are an empath, this kind of experience will probably sound familiar. Some empaths are especially affected by music, being particularly sensitive to changes in pitch and tone. With their vivid imaginations, book-loving empaths lose themselves completely within a story and often become firmly attached to their favorite characters. This effect is amplified even further by films. If you have ever had to stop reading a book or watching a movie because the characters' emotions were too much for you to handle, you are probably more sensitive than the average person. You may prefer to watch the same "safe" films over and over again, or avoid films that contain violent or graphic scenes. Even cartoons or adverts on the TV can affect you in a profound way. A charity campaign featuring victims of abuse, poverty or natural disasters may make you cry, even if you were previously in a good mood. On a related note, consider how generous you are towards others, especially those in pain. Empaths often feel that they have a duty to lessen the suffering of others. When we see that someone else is in need of help, the fact that we sense their pain on a profound level is enough to motivate us to act. We know that others deserve our help, and fully appreciate how much they are hurting.

Your choice of friends can provide you with more clues. First of all, empaths tend to adhere to the "quality over quantity" principle when it comes to socializing. **We often keep in touch with a few close friends and see little point in building an extensive social network for the sake of it.** As empaths are easily overstimulated, they tend to schedule relatively few get-togethers or vacations with family and friends. Provided their self-esteem is sufficiently high, they also believe in holding out for good, solid friendships. Empaths do not reach out to anyone and everyone in the hope of making friends. **We are content in our own company, and if someone doesn't send out the right kind of vibe, we are not interested in wasting our time or theirs!** If you are an empath, you will know exactly how an individual affects you on a psychological level, and tend to avoid those who either leave you overstimulated or drained.

Finally, think about how sensitive you are to sensory input. When you are exposed to strong smells, loud noises, spicy tastes, flashing lights, and rough textures next to your skin, how do you react? Being highly sensitive, empaths often have **very clear likes and dislikes** when it comes to what they wear, see, eat and listen to. In the next chapter, we will look at the science behind sensitivity and empathy and discover why it is that some people are particularly attuned to environmental and interpersonal cues.

Chapter 3: The Science Behind Empathic Abilities

At this point, you may be wondering why some people are born with empathic abilities. In this chapter, I'll introduce you to several scientific theories, experiments and phenomena that may account for high sensitivity and extraordinary empathic abilities. When you understand precisely why you are an empath in the first place, your gifts will seem less mysterious and the prospect of learning how to harness them less daunting. Essentially, empaths have a biological makeup that distinguishes them from the rest of the population. However, there is nothing particularly weird or "spooky" about these differences. It isn't that we have a special, extra empathy organ or extrasensory perception. An empath's abilities can be explained with reference to the same organs and biological processes common to every human – it's just that ours seem to be more sensitive.

We'll start with the mirror neuron system. Have you ever wondered what part of the brain enables us to work out what someone else might be feeling? There is no specific "empathy module." Instead, several parts of the human brain contain cells that grant us the ability to identify with someone else based on their facial expressions and body language. Since it allows us to perceive the emotions of other people by reflecting what they are thinking and feeling in our own minds and bodies, scientists have dubbed it the "mirror neuron system."

This system was discovered by accident. In the 1990s, Italian neurophysiologist Dr. Giacomo Rizzolatti and his team were carrying out experiments with macaque monkeys. At the time, they were not interested in emotion or empathy. Their original aim was to record the activity of individual brain cells that fired when the monkeys performed various movements. They found that, as anticipated, cells in parts of the brain known as the prefrontal and motor cortices fired when the monkeys reached for objects. **What they did not expect to find was that some of these cells fired in the same manner when the monkey merely watched another monkey or human carry out the same movement.**[6]

Later experiments with humans suggested that we have a similar system. For example, a study using brain-scanning technology found that whether people are carrying out finger movements themselves or watching others perform the same gesture, the same parts of the brain become

---

[6] Ferrari, P. F., Gallese, V., Rizzolatti, G., & Fogassi, L. (2003). Mirror neurons responding to the observation of ingestive and communicative mouth actions in the monkey ventral premotor cortex. *European Journal of Neuroscience, 17*(8), 1703-1714.

active. Scientists in this field believe that our mirror neurons not only allow us to feel what someone else might be feeling or how it would feel to carry out a particular action, but also to understand the intention behind an action. **This would have served us well as a species throughout our evolutionary history, enabling us to form strong bonds with others and predict their behaviors.**

What does this mean for those of us looking to understand empathic abilities? Just as people vary in terms of their perceptual abilities, pain tolerance and memory, empaths may have a mirror neuron system that is significantly more active than those of other people. Scientists are not sure what determines the efficacy and sensitivity of an individual's mirror neurons, but it is possible that genetics play a role. Differences in mirror neurons have been cited as a possible underlying cause of Autism Spectrum Disorders (ASD). A defining characteristic of ASD is trouble reading social cues and the intentions of others. It may be that autistic people have a mirror neuron system that is less active than average, or that it may work in a different manner compared with neurotypical people. Based on results of research into autism, it seems entirely possible that highly sensitive people and empaths can also attribute their psychological profile to a specific level of mirror neuron functioning.[7]

Other scientific findings hold the key to understanding the average empath's introverted nature. Specifically, the field of neurology has come up with some useful insights into the typical empath's personality. The human brain contains a variety of chemicals known as neurotransmitters. They are responsible for communicating information between brain cells, which in turn triggers a range of emotional responses. These include feelings of pleasure and satisfaction. Dopamine is essential for feelings of joy and peace. All humans, whatever their personality type, feel better when their brain cells release dopamine. When we engage in stimulating, pleasurable activities such as eating delicious food or laughing with a good friend, our brains release this neurotransmitter. It helps us remember which activities makes us happy. If they trigger the release of dopamine, we are more likely to repeat them in the future.[8]

Psychologists have discovered that introverted people are more sensitive to dopamine than extroverts, which may explain why highly sensitive people and empaths are happy to spend plenty of time alone. **When a little dopamine goes a long way, you don't need much**

---

[7] Rizzolatti, G., & Fabbri-Destro, M. (2010). Mirror neurons: from discovery to autism. *Experimental Brain Research, 200*(3-4), 223-237.
[8] Orloff, J. (2017). The Science Behind Empathy and Empaths. *Psychology Today.*

stimulation to feel excitement and joy – in fact, the kind of stimulation the average extrovert craves triggers such a strong response in an empath's brain that they become uncomfortable at best, and utterly overwhelmed to the point of panic at worst. A loud, crowded party will lift an extrovert's mood, but an empath will receive the same dopamine rush from spending time with just one or two friends. They will also find as much pleasure in creating artwork or reading a good book – activities that will seem "boring" to many non-empaths.

What about an empath's ability to sense a person's mood and character, also known as "heightened intuition"? Looking at research carried out on the human ability to pick up this information at "gut level" is useful. For instance, take the phenomenon of "zero acquaintanceship." Psychologists use the term "zero acquaintance" to describe a situation in which an individual is meeting someone else for the very first time. Researchers working in this field have tried to ascertain what the average person can tell about someone else within seconds of meeting them.

The results are fascinating. One of the first significant papers on this topic was published in 1988 by researchers based at the University of Connecticut.[9] Using a sample of over 250 people, they examined the judgments made by participants regarding the personality of a new acquaintance. They were also interested in whether these judgments actually reflected reality – in other words, they wondered whether the participants were capable of accurately assessing someone else's personality within a short space of time. It turned out that the participants' judgment was fairly accurate when they were asked to rate new acquaintances on conscientiousness and extroversion. These findings, and others published since this study, suggest that humans as a species possess at least some degree of intuition that activates as soon as they interact with someone else. **However, highly sensitive people and empaths seem to have superior abilities in this area.** This may be because they are especially sensitive to body language, which the authors of the study cited above believe is connected with how people express themselves and their personalities.

Finally, empaths may be more likely to experience a neurological phenomenon known as synesthesia. Normally, people experience noises as sounds, light waves entering their eyes as images, and so on. However, people with synesthesia experience a kind of sensory mix-up. For

---

[9] Albright, L., Kenny, D. A., & Malloy, T. E. (1988). Consensus in personality judgments at zero acquaintance. *Journal of Personality and Social Psychology, 55*(3), 387.

example, they may "see" the color yellow when hearing a high-pitched sound, or say that certain shapes elicit distinct tastes. This is hard to imagine for many of us, but synesthetes often say that they spent years oblivious to the fact that other people perceive the world in a manner very different from their own. There is a particular kind of synesthesia that might explain empathic abilities. "Mirror-touch synesthesia" is thought to be an unusual condition in which someone can see another person undergo a physical experience such as coughing or injuring themselves, and feel the sensations as though they were their own. Dr. Joel Salinas, a Harvard-trained physician who has written a book about his medical work, is a mirror synesthete. Whilst working at a hospital, he attended a man who had gone into cardiac arrest. He describes what happened as follows: "I was absorbed in the man in cardiac arrest, fully immersed in his bodily experience. **The sensations in my body mirrored the sensations in his.**"[10]

There is no single, proven theory that explains synesthesia. However, psychologists believe that the strange sensations it causes may be down to "crossed wiring" in the brain. In other words, whilst most people receive information about sight through the visual pathway, sound through the auditory pathway and so on, synesthetes are literally equipped with a different set of connections. In mirror-touch synesthesia, information from the visual pathway (i.e. through the eyes) is somehow translated into sensations of touch and pain. This includes not only visible signs of illness and injury as described by Dr. Salinas above, but also apply to more mundane information such as a person's expression and general demeanor.

Of course, the ultimate theory of empathic abilities may one day encompass all of the above. For example, future research with empaths might show that they have particularly active mirror neuron activity, combined with an especially good eye for subtle interpersonal cues such as facial expression and posture that are not apparent to the average individual. It's also possible that two empaths could possess the same talent but the underlying mechanisms might be different in each case. Whatever the cause, empathic abilities are to be celebrated! In the next chapter, you will learn why it's great to be an empath.

---

[10] Seaberg, M. (2017). Mirror Touch. *Psychology Today*.

Chapter 4: The Upside of Being an Empath

It is normal to feel a little confused or even overwhelmed when you first identify as an empath. This chapter will reassure you that there is nothing to be scared of – being an empath comes with plenty of advantages. **You are blessed with a level of insight that carries with it numerous benefits in social and professional settings.** Although you will face challenges as a result of your gift, the pluses far outweigh the minuses. You should also remember that you are not alone as an empath. Others have walked this path before you and we are more than happy to pass on our experiences.

We'll start with the most obvious advantage of all. As an empath, you are able to understand other people's feelings. Empaths are not always totally accurate in their assessments, but we are right far more often than not. This is a huge asset in familial and romantic relationships. When you can ascertain what your friend, relative or partner is feeling at any moment in time, you come across as caring and considerate. **You are probably an excellent listener, and your talent for interpreting non-verbal cues such as body language and posture means that others feel remarkably comfortable in telling you about their most personal problems.** Since you can readily imagine what it is like to have your secrets given away to others, you will be a loyal friend, partner, and relative. This paves the way for a foundation of trust, which underpins any good relationship.

Your empathic abilities are valuable across a wide range of careers. The most obvious connection to be made here pertains to the medical profession. Should you decide to train as a doctor, for example, your patients will benefit from your excellent bedside manner. However, empaths excel in sectors beyond the caring field.[11] If you have ever had to work under the supervision of a demanding and unsympathetic boss, you will be able to appreciate how far empathy and sensitivity can go in a corporate environment! Empaths know that there is little to be gained from intimidating their subordinates. Instilling fear in junior staff may work in the short-term, but building long-term trust and respect is far more effective. It also creates a more pleasant work environment, which reduces everyone's stress levels – not just those of the empath. If you are an empath with a particular affinity for the arts, consider entering a field that allows you to express this aspect of your personality. This doesn't have to mean working as

---

[11] Aron, E. (1999). *The Highly Sensitive Person.* HarperCollins: London, England.

an artist or a writer. There are plenty of other options. For example, you could work as an arts therapist or as a curator of an art museum.

Empaths are often creative. The connection may not be obvious at first, but consider the effect that emotions have played, and continue to play, in some of the world's greatest works of art. When you consider the complexity of emotion portrayed by artists, writers and directors, you realize that many of them are probably empaths. **Not only do their own feelings inspire them to creative expression, but so do those of other people.** For example, an empath might feel compelled not only to write stories based on their own experiences, but stories based on how they imagine others would have experienced particular events. A painter may set out to depict not only an individual's physical appearance in a portrait, but also to capture their personality or essence. Even if an empath isn't a technically accomplished artist, they will still feel a sense of peace and achievement when they have succeeded in expressing their emotions. **Translating painful feelings and memories onto a page or canvas may not be the most pleasant of experiences, but it is extremely cathartic.**

If you are an empath but do not consider yourself creative, I suggest you have a rethink! I never thought I was remotely "artistic," even though I felt compelled to express my feelings, because I was never any good at drawing. However, my therapist gently pointed out that there are plenty of other approaches to the visual arts. She suggested that I invest in a few cheap canvases, a box of acrylic paints, and simply paint whatever made "sense" to me. I was skeptical, but agreed to give it a try. Within a few hours I was producing abstract art, and loving it! Not everything I paint is amazing, but one of my creations hangs on my cousin's living room wall. She says it "speaks to her," which I take as a great compliment. My art is always inspired by my feelings, and it is a form of therapy for me.

Another advantage of being an empath is an ability to really enjoy the small pleasures of everyday life. As you now know, sensitive people feel the effects of dopamine to a greater extent than others. This means that smelling a lovely bouquet of flowers, going for a brisk walk alone, or having coffee with a trusted friend can be enough to make you smile for hours. Empaths may be vulnerable to sensory overload, but we can turn this to our advantage. A scented candle will smell especially good, and a pet's fur will feel particularly soft.

This brings me to the next plus point – a heightened connection to animals. This is not to say that empaths are somehow capable of communicating in a special way with their pets. It is important to note that there is no scientific evidence in favor of telepathic communication between humans and non-human animals. However, sensitive and empathic people often place a high value on animal welfare. Therefore, we take very good care of our pets and are likely to see them as one of the family. Being so good at picking up on subtle changes in the environment and in others, we quickly realize when a pet is ill or in pain. Sensitive, empathic people are patient and gentle, which can help with the less pleasant aspects of pet ownership such as toilet training and behavioral management. This also applies to parenting. Children – especially when they are young – lack the vocabulary and experience to describe exactly how they are feeling, which can result in frustration and tantrums. Empaths have a distinct advantage when it comes to parenting, as they can ascertain their child's emotional state even without verbal communication. You have probably noticed that other people's children are drawn to you, both literally and emotionally! You may well be the "cool" aunt or uncle that helps your sullen niece or nephew open up about the problems they are having at school, or the person on a train who helps a baby stop crying with just a kind look and a few words. On the other hand, not all empaths love kids. Some sensitive individuals find that children are far too noisy and emotional, which can be overwhelming.

Empaths often have a set of lofty ideals and a strong sense of right and wrong. Being particularly sensitive to all the suffering in the world, we tend to spend more time than the average person thinking about how to make it a fairer place. This spurs many of us to start voluntary work or become activists. Making a difference in the world is especially rewarding for an empath, because we can literally feel the effect we have on others! Sensitive people typically stick up for the disadvantaged, even when their friends and family tell them that there is no point in worrying too much over other people, or that their energies would be better spent elsewhere.

Finally, learning to make the most of your empathic abilities opens the door to self-awareness. It will prompt a journey towards personal growth you would not otherwise have taken. Coming to terms with your high sensitivity will force you to examine how you relate to others, whether your work is a good fit with your talents, and how to take care of yourself on a psychological and physical level. Introspection can be difficult, even painful at times, but you will become stronger as a result. Many people go through life paying little attention to how they and other people think and behave. When you consciously decide to embrace your abilities, you are giving yourself the gift of heightened self-awareness. **This will spill over into all areas of your life, making you a more effective worker, friend, relative, and partner.**

Of course, I would be lying if I said that empaths didn't come up against difficulties from time to time. In the next chapter, you will learn the most common pitfalls awaiting the unwary empath.

Chapter 5: Challenges Empaths Face

Whilst it's true that empaths often have trouble fitting in with other people and sometimes even society at large, I didn't write this chapter to discourage you. **All of the obstacles described here can be overcome.** The trick is to maintain enough self-awareness that you identify problems as they arise and tackle them head-on. You can always learn from your experiences. The second half of this book contains lots of practical strategies you can use to make your life as an empath a little easier, but in this chapter I'll provide you with an overview of the most common issues empaths need to work through in order to lead a happy, balanced life.

The key issue for most of us is emotional overload. When you effortlessly pick up on what other people are feeling, you are at risk of becoming overwhelmed and burned out. This was my main problem for much of my adult life. Unless I take steps to protect myself from other people's feelings, I can soon find myself developing a headache!

People without empathic abilities may not realize that it isn't just negative emotions that leave empaths feeling this way. When myself and other empaths are forced to spend time with groups, even when celebrating a happy event, we quickly succumb to emotion overload. Of course it makes me happy when my friends and family are in a great mood, but parties and raucous evenings out soon tip from "fun" to "too much" for me. **This is why being in a crowded public place is also a challenge.** When dozens of people swirl around and past me, I can't help but pick up on hundreds of different feelings and moods. It becomes hard to know where my own feelings end and those of others begin. Trying to explain this to non-empaths can be a little frustrating.[12]

My therapist told me that empaths typically feel uncertain when it comes to labeling their own mood states, and may even have problems locating a solid sense of self. An unwary empath who doesn't yet appreciate their own abilities may wonder why it is that they can begin the day in a good mood, and yet feel down all afternoon following lunch with a slightly gloomy colleague. **They might start to wonder whether they are going crazy, and why their moods seem to switch for no apparent reason. The good news is that once they spend less time with other people and learn how to handle their emotions, these issues are resolved.** Once an empath is helped to make the connection between other people and their

---

[12] Aron, E. (1999). *The Highly Sensitive Person.* HarperCollins: London, England.

own mood states, they feel a sense of relief. They realize that they are not mentally unbalanced. They are just a person with special psychological and emotional needs.

Empaths are a misunderstood group, and the sense of being "different" can be damaging. Even worse, some adults are quick to minimize, downplay or dismiss a young empath's abilities. This can leave lasting psychological scars that continue to influence the empath's self-image as a teenager and adult. Despite living in a culture that pays lip service to the notion that diversity is valuable, the sad truth is that those with unusual abilities make most people feel uncomfortable. A parent may have their child's best interests at heart, but feel "spooked" by their son or daughter's talent for detecting even unspoken emotions.

This was the case in my own family. My parents could best be described as "normal" and "down to earth." They were not at all prepared to raise an empathic child. I remember one particular incident that really disturbed my mother. I must have been around seven years of age at the time. Her sister Martha had been visiting for a couple of hours. My mother and aunt chatted away happily enough – or so it would seem to a casual observer – whilst I played nearby. Shortly after Martha left, I followed my mother to the kitchen. As she was washing up the cups, I tugged at her skirt and asked, "Why is Aunt Martha sad? She is really sad, isn't she?" My mother was taken aback. I had no way of knowing at the time, but it turned out that Martha had just the day before discovered her husband had been having an affair. Here's the kicker – not even my mother knew! Martha had decided to "put a brave face on it" for a few weeks after that revelation. Her act had my mother fooled, but not me. It wasn't until years later that Mom finally told me the whole story.

Relationships can pose a number of problems. **Although an empath is capable of enjoying deep and meaningful bonds with other people, their good nature means they run the risk of being exploited.** You will have noticed that you are sometimes used as a "negativity dump." Once someone has realized that you are a good listener who finds it hard to turn away anyone who is suffering, they begin to offload their problems onto you. This makes them feel better, but because you feel their pain all too easily, it leaves you feeling drained. For similar reasons, empaths can struggle to stand up for themselves and tend to avoid conflict. **This can lead to resentment in a relationship – you know that a discussion or even an argument would clear the air, but avoid it because you know that it will disturb your equilibrium.** In the short term this may feel like a good solution, but it can mean that important issues go unresolved. Over time, these may snowball until both parties feel frustrated because they are not being "heard" in the relationship.

The parent-child relationship presents its own unique challenges. If you are an empath with children then they will bring you joy, but also a great deal of anxiety. As outlined in the previous chapter, your strengths as a parent include being able and willing to relate to your child. You will always try to provide emotional support and to fix their problems. The downside is that the natural tendency most parents feel to worry about their children is much more pronounced in your case. If a non-empath learns that their child is the victim of bullying, for example, they will feel distressed. An empath will feel not only sad and angry at the situation, but also feel their child's pain. This can be pure agony. As your child moves into adolescence and invariably becomes more volatile and moody, you are at risk of feeling unstable yourself. Teenage mood swings unsettle non-empath parents, but you are particularly liable to feel down when they are upset over a relatively trivial manner, to feel over-excited when they first fall in love, and so on. **Sensitive people also have a special set of requirements when it comes to their jobs and career direction in general.** Working in a noisy environment such as a factory or busy store is unfeasible for empaths who are prone to sensory overload. Interacting with the public on a daily basis might be too distressing, and customer-facing jobs expose an empath to a barrage of emotions that leave them depleted by the end of the working day. **Empaths are usually more successful in jobs that allow them to work in calm, well-maintained environments within a small team.**

Even extroverted empaths may need reasonable adjustments in the workplace. For example, an empath will find it intolerable to work with someone who is always negative and spends much of their time at work complaining to anyone and everyone who will listen. If you are especially sensitive to noises and smells, working in close proximity to someone who likes to talk loudly or wear strong scents can make all the difference between enjoying and hating your job. **There are coping strategies you can use to protect yourself from negative people at work – they are described in the second half of this book.** However, if you are particularly sensitive, then it may be best to choose a career that will give you a high level of control over your exposure to others and their moods. Remember that not all empaths will experience their special abilities in the same way. For some, working with people in need is so rewarding that they choose to tolerate the discomfort or even pain that comes with it. On the other hand, some quickly realize that their own emotions are quite enough to deal with, and pick careers that allow for a lot of lone working. Young empaths just starting out in their working life may need to try a few different jobs and working styles before they know what suits them best.

Health is another common concern among empaths. For various reasons, sensitive people are more susceptible to physical and mental disturbances, particularly if they have not put in place coping strategies to help them navigate the effects of feeling emotions so intensely. In the next chapter, we will look in greater depth at the link between empathic abilities and health problems.

Chapter 6: Empaths & Health

I briefly talked about the kinds of health problems empaths face in the previous chapter, but the topic is so important that it deserves its own section. In the next few pages, you will learn more about why empaths are susceptible to physical and mental health problems, the symptoms to watch out for, and how to seek help. There is no need to worry that you have an especially fragile body or mind – being an empath doesn't mean that you will invariably spend a lot of time in hospital, or are doomed to an early grave! **On the other hand, it's wise to understand why you need to pay more attention than most to your physical and mental health.**

In her book, *The Empath's Survival Guide: Life Strategies for Sensitive People,* Judith Orloff explains that empaths are more prone to a range of health conditions that occur as a result of detecting other people's distress and feeling it within our own bodies.[13] When you think about how humans usually express their feelings, it begins to make sense. You already know that your body language changes as a function of your mood. When you feel happy, your shoulders are relaxed, and your facial muscles soften into a smile. You tend to feel at ease in your body. However, when you are anxious, your shoulders and back stiffen. The muscles in your face tighten as you frown or pucker your mouth. You may also start biting your nails or feeling random aches, pains and itches as your body prepares to fight or flee. If you feel depressed, stressed or anxious on a frequent basis, this will often translate into a constellation of somewhat vague yet persistent problems.

Orloff notes that her sensitive, empathic patients are regularly diagnosed as suffering from fibromyalgia, chronic fatigue, and tension headaches. Whilst her patients' symptoms do often match those associated with these ailments, she emphasizes that in an empath's case they are triggered not by organic, physical causes, but as the direct result of taking on other people's negative feelings and experiencing stress and tension as a result. This is why conventional treatments may not work, or offer only temporary relief. **The underlying problem is not that someone has, for example, inherited their migraines from their parents, but rather than they have yet to learn how to prevent emotional overload.** Lifestyle

---

[13] Orloff, J. (2017). *The Empath's Survival Guide: Life Strategies for Sensitive People.* Sounds True: Boulder, Colorado.

changes that minimize stress and contact with negative people are much more effective for these patients than taking painkillers. For mirror-touch synesthetes, just watching someone else suffer can cause empathic pain. If they are not aware of their condition, a mirror-touch synesthete will be confused as to why they feel such a baffling array of bodily sensations that seem to have no obvious cause. Most of us have never learned that a minority of the population have this ability, so those with this gift may never think to explore the possibility that they have neurological wiring that differs from the norm.

It isn't only other people that can trigger physical symptoms. Sensitive people are prone to react to stimuli that go unnoticed by others. For example, fluorescent strip lighting in supermarkets and offices can be enough to cause a severe headache or sleep disruption. Living or working in a noisy environment also triggers tension within the body. This triggers feelings of stress and, subsequently, the issues outlined above. Changes in the climate can also affect an empath's body. Warm, sunny weather is particularly enjoyable for some empaths, because they are receptive to the mood-boosting properties of sunlight. On the other hand, some empaths are so sensitive to hot temperatures that they will overheat.

Empaths are also vulnerable to mental health disturbances. If they do not harness their gift effectively and learn how to lessen the impact of other people's emotions, they risk developing anxiety, depression, and general feelings of burnout. Orloff states that she often sees patients who have been diagnosed with these common mental illnesses, yet do not find conventional psychiatric treatment (i.e. medication) to be helpful. Just as typical Western treatments for an empath's physical health problems may not fix the true cause of their troubles, **an empath suffering from a mental health issue needs to look at changing their lifestyle if they want to enjoy a greater level of well-being in the future.**

You now know that empaths suffer physical stress when they take on the posture, body language and behaviors of those around them. However, this also works on an emotional level. Most of us think of emotions and body language as working like this: You feel an emotion, and then it "shows" in your face and general demeanor. **In fact, research has shown that the reverse is also true. If you change the way you position your body and facial features, your mood will change accordingly.** Psychologists refer to this phenomenon as the Facial Feedback Hypothesis, because it describes how the body informs the brain of a person's mood state.[14]

This means that an empath who automatically takes on someone else's unhappy mood and expresses it via a sad expression and slumped posture fuels a vicious cycle – they don't only appear sad in response to someone else's despair, but they also perpetuate their own downbeat mood. **Ultimately, if an empath comes into contact with negative people on a regular basis, they will find themselves spiraling into chronic negativity and depression.** If they are seeing a psychiatrist or therapist for their mental distress, the professional in question will need to possess a solid understanding of empathic abilities and how they can foster negativity.

The same principle applies to anxiety. In my case, merely spending a few hours around an anxious person affects my mood in a profound way. They not only make me feel nervous "for them," but my body will begin to show signs of a panic attack. My muscles will tense, I sweat more heavily, and sometimes my breathing becomes labored. Before I learned about empathic abilities, I thought that I was either prone to random panic attacks or was extremely neurotic. **Now I know why I have such a strong reaction to others, I feel less anxious.** If I do catch myself feeling worried for no good reason, I no longer chastise myself for being crazy or too sensitive.

We now have enough research on empaths to say with certainty that this ability definitely increases the risk of health problems. But I want to end this chapter with a note of caution. If you have been suffering from any of the symptoms above, you should pay a trip to your physician even if you suspect that the root cause is your empathic nature. **You may well be suffering from a stress-related illness or symptoms arising from hypersensitivity to your environment, but it is important to rule out organic causes before changing your lifestyle.** If you don't feel as though your regular doctor sees you as anything more than a body to be examined and treated, consult an integrative practitioner who takes time to learn about their patients' emotional health in addition to their physical symptoms.

In an ideal world, all empaths would learn how to monitor and manage their health from an early age. Unfortunately, this is seldom the case. In the next chapter, you will learn the best way to raise empaths in such a way that they honor both their bodies and their special gift.

---

[14] Strack, F., Martin, L. L., & Stepper, S. (1988). Inhibiting and facilitating conditions of the human smile: a nonobtrusive test of the facial feedback hypothesis. *Journal of Personality and Social Psychology*, 54(5), 768.

Chapter 7: Young Empaths

All adult empaths started out as young empaths! Childhood is a critical period for everyone, and an empath's early experiences shape how they relate to others and understand their talents later in life. An empath who is raised with sympathy and tolerance is much more likely to develop into a happy, well-balanced adult than an individual who is dismissed, invalidated, or bullied. This chapter is written for those who parent, care for, or work with, children and adolescents. It explains how you can spot empathic traits in young children, and how best to support them in discovering and using their gifts. If you parent or work with a teenage empath, you may even want to show them this chapter – it could help them feel better about their abilities, and come to terms with their nature as an empath. If you are still in your teens or early twenties, then this section may help you make sense of your experiences.

Young empaths often appear "different" from an early age.[15] Within hours of their birth, it will become apparent that they are particularly affected by sensory input. Empaths are not usually "good" babies who sleep through the night and enjoy robust health. They also exhibit characteristic behaviors that help them avoid emotional overload in a world that seems big and scary. For those that don't know much about empaths, these behaviors can be quite baffling. **The most common behavioral pattern is withdrawal, often referred to as "shyness."** Some children are just naturally quieter than others, and this is perfectly normal. However, for a young empath, shyness is a coping mechanism. By withdrawing from other people, they are protecting themselves from having to feel the emotions of those around them. Some young empaths protect themselves in a different manner. Rather than keeping themselves separate from others – "acting in" – they tend to "act out" instead. This may seem counterintuitive at first, but when you consider what this boisterous, loud behavior actually enables the child to achieve, it makes perfect sense. Unruly conduct serves as a means of exerting control over the environment and the emotions of others. An empath may prefer to cause a disturbance first before anyone else manages to do so, because at least they will be able to predict how those around them will react. This helps them feel safe. These children are in danger of being labeled as suffering from developmental disorders such as ADHD, whereas in fact what they really need is care and understanding. Whilst healthcare professionals such as

---

[15] Orloff, J. (2017). *Is Your Child an Empath? Tips for Raising Empathic Children.* psychologytoday.com

educational psychologists and psychiatrists are well-trained in diagnosing and treating psychiatric disorders, they sometimes overlook the possibility that a child might be highly sensitive, and not actually suffering from any kind of pathology. If a child or adolescent you care for has to see a specialist, make sure that this person is given a full, detailed picture of their patient's usual behaviors. Ideally, they should see a professional who takes a holistic approach to mental and emotional health. A formal diagnosis might be appropriate in some cases, but the underlying explanation may still be enhanced sensitivity.[16]

Some empaths may appear "well-behaved" much of the time, but then occasionally have full-on meltdowns. These look like temper tantrums, but are actually better thought of as emotional explosions. An empath can only tolerate intense emotional stimuli for a certain amount of time before they are forced to express their discomfort. Since they do not have much control over their circumstances compared with older teenagers and adults, their only option might be to scream and cry in an attempt to regain emotional equilibrium. If you know a child who seems stable but is prone to outbursts that don't seem to be triggered by anything in particular, consider the possibility that they might be an empath.

You can then do a little detective work. **When they have their next outburst, think about what was happening in the hours and days before the incident.** Remember that positive occasions can be just as overwhelming for empaths as unhappy events! Therefore, a few busy days leading up to Christmas or a birthday can be as triggering as an illness or stressful family argument. If you pay attention, you will notice that particular events and stimuli cause this kind of response. With a little forward planning, you will be able to prevent outbursts in advance.

For example, if the child tends to have a meltdown after a full day of playing with friends, this is a sign that they cannot tolerate socializing for more than a few hours. In the future, it would be sensible to schedule no more than one playdate in a day.

An empath may use the above mechanisms, or a combination thereof, quite effectively until adolescence. At that point, the rules of social interaction start to shift and they can struggle to adjust. We all know that teenagers are no longer children, yet they are still a long way off adulthood. There is a good biological explanation for this. The part of the brain responsible for forward planning and decision-making, the frontal cortex, does not finish developing until a

---
[16] Ibid.

person's twenties. If you've ever wondered why even intelligent teenagers have trouble acting like reasonable human beings at times, now you know![17]

Although they are often more mature than their peers, an empath's brain will develop at the same rate. They will also go through the same periods of angst and worry as their friends. The trouble is that they will experience even greater emotional turmoil than is typical for an average teenager. If an adolescent doesn't understand why they seem particularly affected by the normal issues all teenagers have to face, they may become self-critical. This sets up a negative precedent for adulthood, because they might develop the habit of putting themselves down for being "abnormal." **This kind of poor self-image becomes entrenched over the years, and can become a real hindrance to personal growth if not addressed.**

Empathic teenagers must contend not only with their own emotional hurricanes, but those of their friends. It is normal and healthy for young people to listen to one another, and to offer support to their friends during difficult times. Unfortunately, young empaths who find themselves feeling everyone's emotions are particularly vulnerable in their teenage friendships. Listening to a close friend's troubles as an adult empath is hard enough, but a teenager will usually be witness to their friends' mood swings, relationship problems, and worries about school on a daily basis. **It's no wonder that sensitive teenagers often choose to be alone, or prefer to spend time only with one or two close friends.**

On the other hand, empathic teenagers can really excel in the art of rebellion as a means of coping with stress. At the same time, their motives are a little different to those of most teens. It is quite common for adolescents as a group to experiment with drugs, alcohol, and other high-risk behaviors. However, most of the time, this is motivated by the desire to exert control over their lives and rebel against their parents. **For empathic teens, substance abuse can serve as an effective means of shutting out the emotional stimuli around them.** Dr. Judith Orloff, the empathy expert, fell into this category. In one of her books, she explains how her ability to feel the pain and suffering of others resulted in alcohol and drug abuse. At that time she did not understand how to process the emotions she was feeling, and used substances

---

[17] American Academy of Child and Adolescent Psychiatry. (2016). *Teen Brain: Behavior, Problem Solving, and Decision Making.* aacap.org

to help her detach from her emotions and fit in with her peers.[18] This was also true in my case during my high school years.

If you know or suspect that you have a young empath in your care, you may wonder how best to support them. Perhaps the most important thing you can do is to provide them with validation. Empaths realize early on that they possess abilities not shared by other children. **Unfortunately, when a child tries to talk about their feelings with a parent or carer, they are often shut down.** This isn't necessarily an act of malice on the adult's part – often, they simply don't know how to react when a child makes an eerily perceptive comment, or appears very sensitive to strong lights and loud sounds. **However, a child who feels invalidated early in life may choose to suppress their gift for fear of being ridiculed. It is always stressful to deny your true nature, and there will come a point at which a closet empath will need to acknowledge who they are.** As I can testify, this often comes during or after some kind of crisis.

A few reasonable adjustments can make a big difference to a young empath's quality of life. For example, if you notice that they become uncomfortable and too stimulated during playdates with two or more children, make sure they can take a timeout whenever they want. If they find it hard to relax at the end of the day, include some soothing elements in their bedtime routine such as a warm bath with calming essential oils. **If you care for an empathic teenager, let them know that you are always willing to listen to their troubles without judgment.** Some teenagers feel that they would rather their parents not know about their innermost thoughts, and if this applies in your situation you should respect their decision. **At the same time, make sure they have access to a safe person or service they can call upon if they need guidance.** If you work as a teacher or in another role in which you take care of children, use this opportunity to instill tolerance and acceptance of others. Be open in acknowledging that some people have special needs and requirements, but make it clear that everyone has something of value to contribute to society. After all, it would be boring if we were all the same! Empathic and non-empathic children alike look to parents and teachers for guidance, so if you model tolerance and a positive attitude towards diversity, they are likely to adopt these values for themselves.

---

[18] Orloff, J. (2017). *The Empath's Survival Guide: Life Strategies for Sensitive People.* Sounds True: Boulder, Colorado.

Chapter 8: Empaths, The Workplace, & Career Choices

By this point, you will appreciate that empaths are affected by everyday stimuli to a much greater extent than neurotypical individuals. An empath's lifestyle choices will be dictated by their gifts and sensitivities. This includes their choice of job and their general career path. In this chapter, you will learn the questions an empath should ask themselves before choosing a particular career. We will also look at the most common problems facing empaths in the workplace. **Even if you do not identify as an empath, this chapter will still be useful if you work with sensitive people.** By making a few small changes, you can respect the needs of your more sensitive colleagues and enjoy better relationships with everyone at work.

To be an empath is to possess a valuable gift, and you might feel as though you have an obligation to share it with the world. When you start reading about the benefits that come with heightened sensitivity, you will come across phrases like "making the most of your abilities," and "sharing your gift with others." It is true that many empaths want to enjoy their gifts and choose a job that allows them to shine. In fact, I've written this book to help other empaths do just that! However, I want to make it clear that there is no rule or law that states you must deliberately embark on a stereotypically empathic or sensitive career. If you prefer a quiet, straightforward kind of life, there is nothing wrong with choosing an undemanding job that pays the bills. Plenty of people, whether or not they are empaths, find fulfillment in hobbies and relationships rather than a career.

At the same time, most of us want a job that offers us some degree of satisfaction, or at least doesn't make us want to bang our head against the nearest wall. **If you are an empath, start by assessing your own unique set of sensitivities.** Some empaths will be able to tolerate a noisy environment, but feel sick at the thought of dealing with the general public day after day. Others will relish the chance to serve people in need – as long as they have learned to keep their emotions in check – but feel uncomfortable working in an office with strip lighting, hard chairs, and other things that could trigger sensory overload. There are plenty of practical steps you can take in order to manage your sensitivities, **but in the long run it is sensible to choose a job that reflects your needs as an empath.** Think about the sort of place in which you would like to work, rather than dwelling on what you cannot do. If you get stuck, look back over your work history to date. **Of all the jobs you have done and all the**

environments in which you have worked, what has felt best for you? What should you avoid in the future?

When it comes to choosing a specific role, you need to pay more attention to detail than the average non-empath. For example, unless you are absolutely desperate to get a job and need to earn money immediately, it's a good idea to ask for a tour of the workplace before you accept an offer. Ideally, you should also ask to be introduced to your potential colleagues. As an empath, you will immediately be able to feel whether the place and the people within it are a good fit for you. **If the environment is far too stimulating or the other employees appear negative and dissatisfied, think twice before signing a contract.** If the person interviewing you will not be responsible for your performance once you are in the role, ask to meet your boss before taking the position. Trust your gut, because if you are an empath, it will usually tell you everything you need to know.

Most people graduate school or college and then begin their careers with little idea of what they want to do when they "grow up." This lack of direction is common in empaths and non-empaths alike, but empaths face a particular challenge if they have not yet come to terms with their abilities. Some do not fully acknowledge their empathic nature until adulthood. School and college can provide a degree of security for some empaths. For example, an empath may adopt the role of the "shy kid" or even the "class clown," both of which can be effective methods for masking how they really feel. The trouble is that these roles rarely translate well to the workplace. If you try to maintain a shy persona at work, you run the risk of being labeled lazy, uncooperative, or a poor communicator. If you attempt to establish yourself as the office clown, you will be perceived as immature and lacking in basic manners. Empaths who have relied on these kind of masks in childhood and adolescence may therefore find it hard to transition to the workplace.

If this sounds familiar, your task is to allow yourself to show your real self at work. This doesn't mean that you need to out yourself as an empath at every opportunity. Rather, it entails having sufficient trust in your abilities and advantages that you show others that empathy and sensitivity can be assets in every field. Dr. Judith Orloff points out that empaths have five distinct advantages that can help them excel at work.[19] Embrace them! First, you will be an excellent contender for management and mentoring roles – which often go hand-in-hand with

---

[19] Orloff, J. (2016). *Is Empathy Helping or Hurting Your Career?* drjudithorloff.com

promotions and more responsibility – because you understand others and can help them make the most of their strengths. Second, empaths are a passionate group of people, and are therefore likely to make each project as successful as possible. Third, empaths are often great at negotiating and diffusing tension if a dispute should arise. This makes us excellent additions to HR departments! Fourth, empaths are usually superb listeners, which in turn means that we can communicate with a range of stakeholders including senior management, subordinates, and clients. **Finally, an empath feels best when they are honest and open about their feelings.** In today's business world, this kind of authenticity is highly valued. It is useful in forming and maintaining working relationships, and inspiring loyalty in both employees and clients.

You should also take into account that most empaths need a job that provides them with intellectual stimulation. It may be possible to compensate for a boring job outside of work, but as an empath you will have a rich inner life and, as a result, find routine rather tedious. Always make sure that you read job descriptions carefully before applying for a position. Ask yourself whether the duties described therein would suit you. Of course, there is no such thing as the perfect job, so don't feel discouraged if you can't find anything that meets your needs. **A role that offers a variety of tasks and the opportunity to let your natural creativity shine through is likely to be a good fit.**

Even when you find a job that suits you, it may be necessary to request reasonable adjustments at work. For example, let's say that the person in the cubicle next to you keeps their radio on at a low level because music helps them to focus. This may prove to be highly irritating and distracting to you. Fortunately, a polite conversation and a few minor adjustments are usually all that is needed in this kind of situation.

Work is a major part of life for most people, but it is also important to consider other aspects of your personal development. In the next chapter, we will look at one of the most intimate elements you should consider working on – your spirituality.

Chapter 9: Empaths & Spirituality

Not all spiritual or religious people are empaths, and not all empaths are spiritual or religious. However, empaths are often introverted and introspective. They spend a lot of time thinking about the meaning of life, why there is so much suffering in the world, and why they are here in the first place. These are big questions, and I am not going to answer them in this chapter! However, it's worth looking at what "spirituality" can mean for an empath, and how they can use their spiritual beliefs to improve their quality of life.

First, I want to clarify what I mean when I use the term "spirituality." This term has traditionally been associated with those who follow some kind of organized religion. Over the past few decades, it has also become a general term for beliefs associated with New Age ideas and theories including reincarnation, "the other side," crystal healing, and so on. There is no scientific evidence that these phenomena exist, and so I suggest that you explore the third meaning of spirituality – **a way of discovering your own sense of existence in relation to life and the universe.**

So, why might spirituality benefit an empath? First, it can provide a refuge from the hustle and bustle of everyday life. Getting into the habit of quiet contemplation, meditation, or prayer is a welcome respite for those who find themselves easily overwhelmed by their own emotions and those of other people. Again, **you do not have to believe in any particular deity or supernatural phenomena to benefit from tapping into your spiritual side**. All you need to do is remain open to the idea of finding purpose and comfort originating from within yourself. No magic or "woo-woo" required!

Second, it can provide a sense of purpose. We empaths are more prone than other people to existential crises – an utter sense of despair and lack of meaning.[20] We tend to wonder why so many people and animals have to experience mental and physical pain. We worry whether we are making a real difference to other people's lives. All this thinking can be highly stressful. In extreme cases, it can even trigger a nervous breakdown or serious mental illness. However, when someone has come to terms with their own view of the universe and their place in it – whether that be a humanist view, a religious view, or something else entirely – they stand a better chance of looking their fears full in the face and finding comfort in difficult situations.

---

[20] Luna, Aletheia. (2017). *Existential Depression, Sensitivity and Soul Loss*. lonerwolf.com

If you do find solace in organized religion, you will have a set of guidelines to fall back on when you find yourself faced with a moral dilemma. This can be a relief if you tend to spend too much time worrying about the potential implications of every single decision you make. I like the teachings of the Buddha, and use them as a kind of moral anchor when dealing with other people. Although I would not call myself a Buddhist and was not raised in the tradition, the Eightfold Path teaching provides a framework by which I live my life. Essentially, the Buddha taught that in order to minimize our own suffering and that of others, we should aspire to the following: Correct action, correct speech, correct livelihood, correct effort, correct mindfulness, correct concentration, correct view, and correct intention.[21] I know better than to work towards perfection – there's no such thing as a perfect human being – but knowing that these principles will always be there helps me stay calm.

Start by examining your own belief system. Do you have particular ideas about the meaning of life, or the moral code you think people should follow? Write out your thoughts on a piece of paper if it will help. Perhaps you do not like the idea of following someone else's belief system, but prefer to pick and mix parts from various philosophies in a way that makes sense to you? **Now consider whether these beliefs help you make sense of the world, and whether they lift you up when you feel low or anxious.** If you are comfortable and happy in your beliefs, that's great!

On the other hand, this exercise might reveal some gaps in your worldview. For example, you might realize that although you are all too aware of the suffering other people endure, you have yet to make sense of why the world is this way. Again, there is no definitive answer here. If there was, the problem of evil would never have become one of the most popular philosophical questions of all time. **It is your job to determine how to explore moral and philosophical issues in a way that helps you.** If you are a member of an organized religion, perhaps you might like to undertake some formal study of religious texts. If you lean towards a materialist outlook, pick up a few books by philosophers who share your stance. Joining a community that enables you to talk with others who share your views, whether in person or online, can also be helpful. If the first one you join doesn't quite fit, try another.

Once you have taken an inventory of your beliefs and decided where and how they need to be developed, think about ways in which you can build a sense of connection to the world around

---

[21] BuddhaNet. (2017). *The Eight-Fold Path*. buddhanet.net

you. This is another component of spirituality – the idea that every person and object co-exist in the same universe and impact on one another. Spending time in nature, volunteering to help others, building relationships with positive individuals, and appreciating the people, places and events that have brought you to this point in your life are all means by which you can improve your self-awareness. Mindfulness and meditation are also valuable means by which you can create some psychological and emotional "breathing space." There are now lots of good books and websites to help you get started if these appeal to you.

Finally, I want to caution those empaths who do believe in the afterlife, sometimes known as "the other side." You should be aware that there are plenty of people out there who will happily take advantage of your good nature and tell you whatever you want to hear for the sake of making money. For example, some self-styled "psychic mediums" prey on sensitive and empathic people who desperately want to get in touch with deceased friends or relatives. Think very carefully before employing anyone offering such a service. No matter how earnest they are or whatever claims they make, trust your own judgment. Use your empathic abilities to discern whether they are really trying to help, or just want you to open your wallet. The same warning also applies if you are dealing with anyone who promises to "heal" you, whether it be via crystals, Reiki, or some form of alternative medicine.

Trust that you have everything you need to develop your own spirituality, whatever that may mean to you. It will help you build on your self-awareness, which is a valuable asset for empaths and non-empaths alike. In the next chapter, we'll look at self-awareness from another angle.

Chapter 10: Empaths & Emotional Intelligence

Perhaps you have taken an IQ test at some point in your life, but how much thought have you given to your EQ? First popularized by Daniel Goleman in the mid-1990s, the concept of emotional intelligence (EQ) refers to someone's ability to identify and respond appropriately to their own emotions and those of other people. It has nothing to do with intellectual ability, more commonly referred to as "IQ" (Intelligence Quotient).[22] **There are plenty of people out there who excel at intellectual tasks, yet find it hard to relate to other people or manage their own feelings.** Likewise, we all know some individuals who are very empathic, yet have never been high achievers at school or in their work.

You'd be forgiven for assuming that the average empath must possess a high EQ. Research has shown that EQ does indeed correlate with the ability to feel empathy, so this conclusion has some basis in fact. However, emotional intelligence is not just the ability to know exactly how others feel. **It is a complex set of skills that, when combined together, set you up for happy relationships with others.** As a bonus, they also let you enjoy a good relationship with yourself. Emotionally intelligent people accept who they are, and learn how to manage their own moods. In this chapter, you will learn what emotional intelligence really means, and how to identify gaps in your own EQ skill set.

The good news is that everyone can improve their EQ, as long as they are willing to put in the practice. Self-awareness is the first step towards self-improvement. This information will stand you in good stead for the second half of this book, which will help you not only live a happier life as an empath but also build up your EQ.

"Emotional intelligence" and "empathy" are used interchangeably in some conversations around empaths and sensitive people, so it is important that you hold a good understanding of this concept.

We'll begin by differentiating between the two core components of emotional intelligence.[23] Each is associated with a distinct set of skills. When you look closer, it turns out that EQ is more complex than it first appears! One component of EQ is commonly referred to as "Social Competences." It is here that empaths tend to excel. Empathy is a major theme in the Social

---

[22] Goleman, D. (2005). *Emotional Intelligence: Why It Can Matter More Than IQ*. New York, New York: Bantam Books.
[23] Skills You Need. (2017). *Emotional Intelligence*. skillsyouneed.com

Competences category. In Goleman's model, empathy entails understanding other people, helping people develop so that they fulfil their potential, possessing an ability to understand the value of diversity, and the ability to pick up on nuances in social situations. Social Competences also include the act of building bonds, working as part of a team, communicating with others, and using our ideas to influence people.

The other component of emotional intelligence is "Personal Competences." This refers to how we handle our own thoughts and feelings. Within this set of competencies, we have self-awareness, self-regulation, and motivation. To be self-aware is to know how we are feeling, why are feeling this way, and to have confidence in our self-assessment. Self-regulation entails knowing how to exert self-control, how to behave in an ethical, conscientious manner, and how to adapt to new situations. Finally, the "motivation" element addresses our drive for achievement, our capacity for optimism, and willingness to use our own initiative.

As you read the above descriptions, you probably realized that you are strong in some areas and relatively weak in others. That's OK – everyone has a unique profile, and no-one can put these skills into practice all the time. For example, you might have excellent self-control, but struggle to remain optimistic. Or you may be like me, and feel confident in working as part of a team, but sometimes have trouble adapting to new situations.

You may also have realized that the typical empath will have trouble with a few of these skills if they have not mastered the art of gaining control over their emotions. Self-awareness and self-regulation are only possible when we appreciate what we are feeling, why we are feeling it, and the importance of knowing how to control ourselves. Sensitive people tend to spend a lot of time worrying about how other people are feeling, and pour precious energy into trying to solve other people's problems. Worse, we don't always realize that this is what we're trying to do! Needless to say, it doesn't work very often. We have to respect that other people have to live their lives in a way that suits them. **Ironically, we empaths can be very sensitive to what other people are feeling, but less aware when it comes to how we process this information.** Empaths can feel someone else's pain so acutely that their natural inclination is to find a practical solution.

This then raises the issue of self-regulation. Having quickly figured out that someone is anxious or depressed, our first instinct might be to ask, "What's wrong, exactly?" The trouble is that, much of the time, people attempt to hide their feelings for a good reason. Just because we can feel the emotions that others want to keep hidden doesn't mean that we should act on that information. To be emotionally intelligent, we don't just need to empathize with someone – **we need to be selective in what we do with that information.**

In my early twenties, I worked with a woman who had recently married. I knew that a few people had jokingly asked her when she was planning to start a family with her new husband, and she always replied that they both wanted to work for a couple more years before having children. One day, several members of the department were in the coffee room talking about a meeting we were scheduled to attend later that day, and a project we were all working on. No-one else in the room seemed to notice anything was up, yet I suddenly realized that my coworker seemed much more excited and on edge than usual. For a few seconds I ran through several theories – She was getting a promotion? Moving house? – and then it hit me! She was pregnant. I was so excited on her behalf that before I knew what I was doing, I asked, "Are you sure you're going to wait a while to start a family?" Her face completely drained of color. Silence descended over the room. Needless to say, I was correct, but I should definitely have waited until we were alone before bringing it up.

Motivation and maintaining a sense of optimism can also be hard for empaths. Because we understand all too well how much suffering there is in the world, we can find it hard to keep hoping that things will change. Connecting with other empaths and trying to look out for the positives along with the negatives are good first steps too. **Optimism is a skill like any other. When you take the decision to choose optimism over pessimism, you will find negativity easier to deal with, whether it be in yourself or in others.**

Finally, teamwork and building bonds with others can be a challenge. Your conscientious, sensitive nature means that you are an asset to any team, but working with especially negative or dominant people can cause you problems. If you have had bad experiences with teamwork in the past, this might be enough to prompt you to shut down entirely in order to protect your sanity! However, working with others is an essential skill for those working in almost all sectors, so it is in your best interests to master it. The techniques outlined in the second part of this book will help you do just that. You may never enjoy being thrown into a group, but you can certainly become more competent in this area.

It takes time, effort and experience to improve your emotional intelligence. However, we should strive to develop our gifts, because the world needs us more than ever. In the next chapter, I'll explain why.

Chapter 11: Why The World Needs Empaths

I'm going to close the first half of this book with a discussion on why the world needs empaths more than ever before. We aren't the easiest group of people to understand, and we definitely have special requirements. But at the same time, we have always needed, and will always need, especially sensitive people in every society. In this chapter, I'll explain what empaths can offer society, and why they should be accorded plenty of respect for their skills.

We live in an increasingly globalized world. Communication has never been easier – it is just as simple to make contact with someone on the other side of the world as it is to talk to someone on the other side of town. Obviously, this has many advantages. We can stay in touch with family and friends at virtually no cost, and we can work from any location. Cheaper travel and a globalized workplace means that most of us have opportunities that would have been unthinkable just a couple of generations ago.

However, with increased contact and global movement comes a greater risk of tension and conflict. Some people welcome globalization as a chance for cultures to exchange ideas, but many would prefer a world in which people kept their ideas to themselves. Unfortunately for them, there is no going back. All we can do is attempt to develop an understanding of other people's viewpoints and accept them for who they are, whilst working towards a peaceful global community. Empaths are exactly the kind of people the world needs if we are going to be a truly inclusive, multicultural society. Sometimes, other people's actions and beliefs can seem baffling, but if you are an empath then you have a head start. We are better than most at looking beyond sensationalist media. Because we cannot help but want to understand how others feel, empaths are tolerant and respectful. This does not mean that we want to be treated like doormats, happy to silence our own voices whilst letting others speak up. **It simply means that we are interested in getting to know people as individuals, not just as a member of a stereotyped or maligned group.**

The advent of the internet has triggered another set of problems across many societies, because it has highlighted the ugly side of human nature. Never before have individuals been able to make their private thoughts public in such a way that they face no consequences for hurting other people's feelings. Unfortunately, the internet seems to encourage an outpouring of petty gossip, slander, and even outright hatred from some quarters. If you have ever received cruel comments on any of your social media posts or something innocent you posted to a forum, you will know how soul-crushing this kind of bullying can be. For some reason, it can be even more hurtful when it comes from someone who doesn't know us. We can find ourselves thinking, "Well, if a complete stranger feels compelled to point out my flaws, they must be really bad! What must my family and friends be saying about me behind my back?"

Empaths make for responsible internet users, and they can lead the way in shaping a more compassionate online community. You are unlikely to find an empath leaving unkind comments on social media, or trolling an online forum. They are all too aware what it is like to feel psychologically attacked and emotionally overwhelmed. **Instead of using the internet to spread negativity, they see it as a tool for promoting inspiring messages, spreading thought-provoking media, and connecting with other sensitive individuals.** When I was researching empaths and sensitivity for the first time, I really appreciated some of the blogs I found about living well as an empath. For the first time, I felt as though other people really knew how I felt! If you have a few hours to spare, why not consider setting up your own blog? There are lots of other empaths out there who would appreciate learning from your experiences. Moreover, the comments section will usually be full of kind, empathic people who want to express their thanks and reach out to other empaths.

The state of our environment is another reason why the empaths among us have much to offer society. As you know, empaths are highly attuned to external stimuli. We notice when things look different, wrong, or out of place. This includes not only our immediate environment, but the natural world in general. **Sensitive people tend to worry about the state of the earth**. We know all too well that polluting rivers and felling trees not only make the world an uglier place in which to live, but also have an adverse effect on human beings. We read news stories about victims of natural disasters – many of which are caused by climate change – and know that the human race needs to work hard to contain the damage we have caused. This sense of urgency and compassion for others is a great motivator for those of us who want to get involved in charity work and campaigning.

Empaths are also drawn towards causes that aid abused people and animals. We can imagine what victims of abuse go through, as we have tapped into sorrow and pain all too often in our lives. Some charity campaigns on TV can reduce us to tears within seconds. This is an uncomfortable way to live at times, but feeling as though you have made a difference is highly rewarding. I send regular donations to a children's charity and also "sponsor" a dog at my local shelter. **It might not be enough to change the world on a grand scale, but I strongly believe that everyone should play their part and help wherever possible.**

With the rise of the media, we are being exposed to more advertising than ever before. Adverts subtly – or not so subtly – tell us why our lives are not OK exactly as they are, and what we should buy in order to feel better about ourselves. **Most people like to think that they are somehow immune to the effects of advertising, but in reality, too many of us rack up credit card debt trying to emulate a particular lifestyle.** This kind of materialism encourages competition and a tendency to judge other people based on where they buy their clothes, how much they earn, and the sort of car they drive. Consumerism isn't just bad for the planet. It also encourages a lack of empathy. Mass-market products are often made by poor people in underdeveloped countries who earn very little money for their labor, but this fact is never mentioned by large corporations! We are encouraged to just accept the idea that exploiting other people for our own material gains is natural, normal, and inevitable.

Sensitive people are likely to see through the system and try to correct these injustices. Some may make changes to their purchasing habits, and encourage family and friends to do the same. An empath may go even further and set up their own ethical business or charity with the intention of helping those mistreated in the name of corporate greed.

Finally, I want to mention a change that affects us all on a daily basis. Gender roles are changing in our society, and we need empathic people to help ease the transition. Men and women alike feel uncertain about their place in the world. Women have more opportunities than ever before to succeed in the workplace, but they still feel conflicted about balancing career and family. They are also more likely to take on more than their fair share of the housework, even if both they and their partner are in full-time employment. Men also face problems. Most of us pay lip service to the notion that men should be allowed to express their emotions, but in practice many do not feel as though they can truly "open up," even among close family and friends. Men may also feel confused about what women want from them in romantic relationships. Now that women can earn their own money and make a name for themselves in business, the idea that men should always make the first move and pay for dates is ridiculously old-fashioned – or is it? Some people prefer to stick to more traditional gender roles, whereas others find them offensive.

We are in a strange period of flux, and it's hard for everyone to know exactly where they stand. **The answer is to practice clear communication in relationships, but this isn't**

always easy. Empaths are at an advantage here, because they are able to detect what anyone is feeling, regardless of their gender. If everyone made a point of being more empathic when dating, lots of us would be in happier relationships! I have always been the friend in my social circle others have come to for relationship advice, and if you are an empath, you have probably found yourself in a similar role. We are always ready to listen, empathize and offer advice to friends and family who are having trouble with their partners. In the next chapter, you will learn how to balance your emotions whilst empathizing with other people.

Part II

Chapter 12: Working with Your Emotions & Staying Balanced

You know by now that empaths have a great gift, but at the same time, **it's vital that you learn how to deal with your own emotions.** The second half of this book provides you with lots of tips and strategies that will help you do just that. We're going to start with the basics – how to identify and channel your emotions so that they don't throw you off balance. If you struggle with anxiety or depression, these techniques will help you feel less overwhelmed on a day-to-day basis.

The first tip I'm going to suggest may surprise you. Over the next few days, **I suggest you start labeling your emotions as you feel them.** This takes a bit of effort, but consider this: Just because you are good at detecting what others might be feeling, **this doesn't mean that you are automatically skilled in processing your own emotions.** If you can't quite put your finger on what you are feeling and why, you are in danger of confusing your emotions with those of other people. This can lead to a sense of imbalance. To keep your sanity, you need to become sufficiently self-aware that you know exactly how you feel, and how others affect your mental state.

Every time your mood changes, take a moment to register how you were feeling before the shift took place, and what you are feeling right now. Can you pin down what happened? In some cases, there will be an obvious reason behind the switch. For example, you might have opened your email inbox and received a request from your boss, who wants you to work several hours of overtime this weekend. For empaths and non-empaths alike, this would be enough to spoil a good mood. If you had to wait on the phone for 20 minutes to speak to a representative from your bank, you'd probably feel annoyed. Again, this is normal. These incidents would affect most people in the same way, regardless of their empathic abilities.

For an empath, it's more important to identify those times when your mood has been altered as a result of interacting with other people. Once you can identify the cause, you are then in a good position to think about precisely what triggered the feelings. For instance, suppose you have had a great morning at work, but after coming back from lunch with a colleague, you feel irritable for several hours for no obvious reason. If you carried out the exercise above, you would first label this feeling as "irritable." You would then cast your mind back over the day's events and realize that the only thing that could have changed your mood was the lunch with your coworker. Empaths are so good at picking up on other people's feelings, we might not even notice and label it at the time, which isn't necessarily a positive habit.

Think about how the other person spoke, whether you picked up on any tension in their posture, and consider whether they were trying to suppress their emotions. Did their actions and words match? To continue with the above example, you might think back over your lunch and recall that your colleague was sitting up straighter than usual, and that they smiled less often. These cues would have indicated that your colleague was feeling on edge. As an empath, you would have felt her irritation, and carried it with you into the afternoon. **Within a few days of practicing this exercise, you will find that other people's feelings exert less of an impact on your own mood.** It all comes down to self-awareness and making a commitment to understand yourself.

The next step is to consciously label the emotions you pick up from others in "real time." This requires a little concentration, but it helps you separate your "stuff" from their "stuff." For example, if you begin a conversation with someone in a contented state of mind and they begin to show signs of anger, your natural reaction as an empath is to feel their rage. You might feel your inner peace slip away, your chest tightening, and perhaps your fists might start to clench as your emotions resonate with theirs. You are certainly empathizing with them, and this will help them feel understood, but it comes at the cost of your emotional health!

By quickly labeling their feelings, and keeping a running commentary as their face and body changes to reflect their shifting emotions, you are drawing a line between yourself and the other person. It will also help you realize that all feelings are transitory. Even if you feel very sad or angry, it will pass – and this applies to other people as well. This is helpful if you have the common empathic habit of worrying too much about other people's problems. Notice that everyone's feelings ebb and flow. **You don't have to assign yourself the task of cheering someone up when they are down**. Trust that they will either take care of themselves, or at least that their feelings will change.

You also need to learn the art of balancing your own emotions. I believe that everyone should learn how to identify and work with their feelings as a child – maybe it should even be on the school curriculum – **because it would save so much angst later in life.** If you know exactly how to lift your spirits when you are low, **other people's emotions will lose their power over you because you know that you always have the option of making yourself feel better.** It sounds so obvious, doesn't it? You'd think that all of us would take the time to make our personal happiness a priority. After all, you cannot feel positive about your life otherwise! The sad truth is that the demands of our busy lives mean that basic self-care often comes at the expense of working at a job, taking care of a family, or both. Luckily, you can figure out what makes you feel good, and then do those things on a regular basis. You don't have to earn these treats, or enjoy them only when you have ticked everything off your to-do list. As self-help author Richard Carlson says in his classic book *Don't Sweat The Small Stuff,* your inbox will never be empty.[24] There is no point in trying to get everything done. You need to strike a balance between work and play. You deserve to feel good simply because you are a worthwhile human being, and you cannot hope to function at your best if you do not take responsibility for your own happiness.

There are a few simple tips and tricks you can use on a daily basis to keep yourself calm and contented. Yoga teacher and author Kino MacGregor recommends **slowing down and reminding yourself of what is going well in your life.**[25] This gratitude exercise will quickly improve your mood, and make you less vulnerable to other people's negativity. She also recommends **taking a timeout from an overwhelming situation** in order to get some emotional distance. Moving to another room or spending a few minutes outside can be enough to help you regain emotional equilibrium. In MacGregor's words, it helps you "remain objective" even in challenging situations. Deep breathing is also soothing and helps maintain normal oxygen and carbon dioxide levels in the body, which is essential for preventing symptoms of panic attacks. When worry strikes, take a few deep breaths. Pay attention to how the air flows in and out of your body.

If you have a lot of strong emotions that you want to release, consider journaling. Studies have shown that writing about your feelings, particularly if they are negative or linked to a traumatic event, helps restore emotional health.[26] It doesn't work for everyone, but what have you got to lose by giving it a try? Find a notebook that appeals to you and write out your innermost thoughts and feelings. There are apps and websites that provide password-protected online journals, but I personally think there's something particularly satisfying about using an old-fashioned pen and paper. Once you have vented your negative feelings, destroy your piece

---

[24] Carlson, R. (1996). *Don't Sweat the Small Stuff...and It's All Small Stuff: Simple Ways to Keep the Little Things from Taking Over Your Life.* New York, New York: Hyperian.
[25] MacGregor, K. (2014). *9 Easy Tips for Emotional Balance.* huffingtonpost.com
[26] Lepore, S.J., & Smyth, J.M. (2002). *The Writing Cure: How Expressive Writing Promotes Health and Emotional Well-being.* Washington, DC: American Psychological Association.

of paper. Burn or shred it. As you do so, think about how much better you will feel without those negative thoughts dragging you down. This exercise sends a clear message to your subconscious mind – "You don't need to think about this stuff any longer." It will also stop you from reading back over what you have written, and encourage you to look to the future instead. You might want to repeat this exercise several times, until you feel better.

Next, start using your journal to record the positive events in your life. Why is this such a powerful tool? Generally, revisiting past hurts will only make you feel worse. It is healthier in the long run to focus on what is going well, the things that are making you happy, and your personal development. **There is a sound biological reason that explains why accentuating the positive will boost your quality of life.** It's all related to the Reticular Activating System (RAS). Basically, the RAS is a part of the brainstem that serves as a link between your conscious and subconscious thoughts. Thanks to the RAS, your conscious thoughts trickle down into your subconscious mind.[27]

You have probably already experienced the power of your RAS. For example, have you ever considered buying a particularly unusual brand of car, only to suddenly start seeing these cars everywhere you go? Your RAS controls what you notice in your environment, and what you think about. Another common example is that of pregnant women suddenly noticing children wherever they look!

This effect can work in your favor, or it can make your life miserable. It all depends on how you use your RAS. If you spend a lot of time thinking about everything that has gone wrong in your life and doubting your capabilities, you are priming yourself to experience low self-esteem and regret. You condition yourself to notice everything that is "bad," whilst overlooking the positive moments. On the other hand, if you focus on positive events, you are setting up your subconscious help you feel good. Of course, you need to take action in order to improve your life, but learning to employ your RAS is the perfect foundation for success.

Finally, you need to be realistic when it comes to arranging your social life. Our society places a lot of value on being a popular, sociable person with a full calendar. Therefore, you might fall into the trap of thinking that your status will improve if you fill up your schedule. Some empaths are happy to socialize frequently, but the majority finds that noisy gatherings and large events are too stimulating. Be honest with yourself. If you struggle to tolerate social events for more

---

[27] Bokhari, D. (2015). *The Power Of Focusing On What You Want.* meaningfulhq.com

than a couple of hours, work with your limitations. As you implement the techniques in this book you might expand beyond these limitations, but do not push yourself to the point of discomfort. **Accept that empaths often need lots of time alone, and that your friends should understand that this is just how you are.**

All these techniques can help sensitive, empathic individuals stay in balance. However, if you are in a lot of emotional distress, it is a good idea to seek the help of a therapist, a psychiatrist, or both. In the next chapter, I'll give you two other tools that will help you stay emotionally balanced and enjoy healthier relationships with family, friends, and colleagues.

Chapter 13: The Importance of Setting Boundaries & Asserting Yourself

You already know why it is vital for an empath to work on their EQ and distinguish their own emotions from those of other people. In this chapter, we are going to take a closer look at two other tools that can help you sort out where your emotional "stuff" ends, and that of other people begins. First, we'll look at how setting boundaries will ensure you are not overloaded by the feelings and demands of other people. We will then look at assertiveness, and why it can help you reinforce boundaries and keep your emotions under control.

First, we're going to look at boundaries. So what exactly does this term mean? Think of a personal boundary as being like a fence, the kind that a farmer might build to stop someone trespassing on their property and stealing their livestock. A boundary is the psychological equivalent. It allows you to interact with other people in a way that feels safe and manageable. **A boundary allows you to say, "This is what I will and will not tolerate from others. This is the minimum level of respect that I deserve to receive as a human being."**

You can also set boundaries with yourself. For example, you can decide not to dwell on other people's thoughts and emotions. Empath and writer Jenn Bovee repeats the following to herself whenever she interacts with others: "I am unwilling to absorb anyone else's energy. I want to be aware of it, but I'm unwilling to absorb it." In this context, "energy" doesn't necessarily have any spiritual meaning. Bovee is referring to the feelings she picks up from other people, and how she prevents herself from becoming overwhelmed by their emotions.[28]

This is a valuable tool for empaths, because we tend to end up as emotional sponges or "feeling dumps" for other people. Sometimes this is a good thing. It is a great feeling to know that you have listened to someone else's problems and allowed them to feel heard. The trouble starts when we lose the ability to control how their woes affect us. **Deciding in advance what your boundaries are gives you peace of mind.** You will know exactly when you need to change the topic of conversation, or even when to leave if the emotional intensity is too high.

Boundaries will be different for each empath. Some of us are capable of listening for longer than others, and our boundaries must reflect our individual personalities and tolerance for others. You can base boundaries on gut feelings, objective numbers, or both. For example, if you are

---

[28] Bovee, J. (2017). *Boundaries for Empaths.* huffingtonpost.com

comfortable relying on your instincts, you could set yourself boundaries like "I will talk to someone until I start to feel tense," or "I will happily interact with someone until they make me feel as though they are taking advantage of my willingness to listen." If you would prefer to set boundaries based on objective measures, you could set boundaries such as "I will not let anyone complain to me about their problems for more than half an hour," or "I will not answer any calls or messages after dinner, unless it is an emergency."

Your boundaries will also be different depending on who you are talking to, and in what context. For instance, you might find that it's relatively easy to talk to your siblings about whatever is going on in their lives, but that conversations with your parents drain you quickly. Therefore, you may choose to limit the number of times you visit or talk with your parents. Of course, you can change your boundaries at any time. You might go through phases in which you feel more capable of dealing with people and their issues, and your boundaries can expand or contract to reflect these shifts.

You don't need to gather all your friends and family in one room and give them a comprehensive outline of your boundaries, but it's a good idea to be clear on **what you expect and tolerate from other people**. When you set out boundaries in positive terms, others are more likely to respect them. For instance, suppose you have a friend who you love dearly, yet at the same time tends to waste your time by telling you about their problems over and over again. You could tell them that you are happy to listen, but that within half an hour you think it would be a good idea to start talking about happier topics. If that didn't work, you would have to be a little blunter. A statement such as, "You know, I don't think this is helpful. Let's talk about something else" would make your boundaries crystal clear.

Unfortunately, some people will deliberately overstep your boundaries, no matter how clearly you communicate. Sometimes this is because they are socially inept, and sometimes it is because they are malicious or have a misplaced sense of entitlement. Either way, your best defense against violations of your boundaries is assertiveness. Assertiveness is the fine art of standing up for your wants and needs. An assertive person does not let other people dictate the outcome of a situation, but neither do they use intimidation or bullying tactics to get what they want. It's about recognizing that everyone has the right to have their wishes and opinions respected (within reason, of course). All of us are entitled to decide our own boundaries, and have the right to be treated as human beings worthy of respect. What does this look like in practice? We're going to take an everyday social situation, and then look at how a passive person, an aggressive person, and an assertive person would respond.

Imagine this scenario. You get home from a long, busy day at work. The afternoon was taken up by meetings, and you are suffering from emotional overload. You know that the best way to pass the evening is to relax, take a long bath, and read a good book. In short, you are in no mood for any social interaction. Just as you put your dinner in the oven, the phone rings. You have recently set a boundary when it comes to late evening calls – you won't take them unless it's an emergency. Caller ID shows that it's your friend Jane. You like Jane, but recently she has been complaining to you about her father, who has been pestering her to find better job, get married, and "settle down." Jane's grievances have already taken up a few hours of your time over the past two weeks. The last thing you want to do is spend the evening listening to her complain. What should you do in this situation?

If you took a passive approach, you would end up listening to your friend moaning about her family problems for at least an hour. You wouldn't be able to enjoy your dinner, and after the call you would probably feel resentment towards Jane. Even worse, you might feel guilty for feeling annoyed, despite the fact that your evening would have been ruined.

If you took an aggressive approach, you'd snap at Jane and tell her that you'll call her back when it's a more convenient time. This would certainly reinforce your personal boundary, but it would also harm your friendship.

The best way to handle a situation like this is to be assertive. If you were to take an assertive stance, you would tell Jane that you care about her and want to help, but you are currently in no position to give her support. You would gently but firmly tell her that she could expect to hear back from you tomorrow. By responding in an assertive manner, neither of you would feel disrespected. **Assertive people strive to balance their own needs with those of other people. As an empath, you need to master this skill.** Otherwise, even those closest to you will violate your boundaries. If you do not assert yourself, others will conclude that you don't mind acting as their emotional punching bag.

Sometimes, people will become upset when you stand up for your needs and defend your boundaries. This will be hard for you to take the first few times, because you will feel as though you have upset another person. You need to remember that if you have behaved like a reasonable adult, you have already met your obligations. **It's up to the other party to decide whether they want to accord you the same respect in return.** If they do – great! If they decide to throw a tantrum or give you the silent treatment, this says more about their maturity (or lack thereof) than your social skills or character. Your family, friends and colleagues might be surprised or even shocked if you start asserting yourself after acting like a doormat for years, but most of them will get used to it. Finally, even if you upset someone else when defending a boundary, you are actually doing them a favor. In order to build good relationships with others, everyone needs to understand the importance of personal boundaries. **Standing up for yourself and insisting that others respect your needs sets a good example.**

Setting boundaries and keeping them firmly intact is a vital tool in protecting yourself from negative energy. However, sometimes you will still find yourself picking up on other people's anger, anxiety and sadness. In the next chapter, you will learn how to deal with negative energy.

Chapter 14: Detecting & Clearing Negative Energy

Some people, places and situations are enough to leave anyone feeling drained and tired. For example, an employee forced to sit through a three-hour meeting at work in a stuffy conference room is likely to go home feeling washed-out. This feeling of heaviness, overwhelming fatigue, and sheer negativity can be termed "negative energy." Note that this term doesn't have New Age connotations in this context. I'm not referring to "dark energy" or "auras," just that unmistakable sensation of being very tired, depleted, and in need of a rest.

As we are so attuned to our surroundings and other people's moods, empaths are especially prone to the effects of negative energy. Over time, it may damage your health. Fortunately, you can use a few simple techniques to detect and clear away negative energy before it starts impacting your vitality. In this chapter, you will learn how to establish whether you are carrying excess negative energy, and how to get yourself in a more positive frame of mind.

The simplest and most effective way of identifying negative energy is to check in with your body. When you feel depressed or angry, your body becomes tense. For example, when you are sad, you are likely to sit slumped over. When you are angry, you may clench your jaw and screw your hands into fists. It doesn't matter whether these feelings are truly your own, or those you have picked up from other people – your body acts as a barometer for your emotions. **As a general rule, the more tension you can feel in your body, the more negative your energy.** A headache that feels as though someone is tightening a band around your head and over your eyes is a sure sign of negativity. Merely thinking about stress-inducing events, even if they took place years ago, can be enough to trigger physical symptoms.

As well as checking in with your muscles and assessing your posture, pay some attention to your digestive system. When we are under stress, our digestive system speeds up. This results in quicker elimination, which means more trips to the bathroom. You might also notice symptoms of indigestion and heartburn. If you are really stressed, you might even feel sick. From an evolutionary standpoint, this is a useful adaptation. Back when we lived simpler lives and had to hunt for food, we would sometimes have to run away from dangerous animals. Rapid elimination would have helped us move more quickly. This old reflex still kicks in today, despite the fact that most of the threats we now face are emotional and psychological rather than physical in nature. Highly sensitive people are prone to ailments and conditions that worsen under stress, such as Irritable Bowel Syndrome (IBS) and eczema.[29] If your symptoms suddenly become worse over the course of a few hours or days, this is a good indication that you have been exposed to an unusually high level of negative energy. Once you have cleared it away, you should find that your health is restored.

Negative energy can also manifest itself as bleak thoughts. I sometimes notice that spending time with a negative person not only leaves me feeling physically tired, but also makes me more pessimistic about life in general. The next time you feel uncharacteristically negative, think back over the last few hours. Chances are that you spent time with someone who was in a downbeat mood. When you pick up on someone else's sadness or anxiety, your thoughts begin to reflect this shift. You may find yourself dwelling on past mistakes, or feeling anxious about potential disasters that could occur in the future. In severe cases, you might have a full-on panic attack. During a panic attack, feelings of anxiety and worry reach a peak. This is accompanied by a range of symptoms that may be severe and frightening in nature. They include shortness of breath, light-headedness, nausea, sweating, and feelings of impending doom. If you do not usually suffer from this problem, these symptoms are a clear sign that you may have tapped into someone else's anxiety.

So what should you do if you have picked up some negative energy? The simplest method is to deliberately release any excess tension within your body. Go for a brisk walk, do some stretches, and take a few deep breaths. Laughter is also effective as a means of releasing tension, so keep a few funny videos or comic strips on hand in case you need a shot of positivity. When you laugh, the muscles in your chest and abdomen get a thorough massage, and the endorphins in your brain provide you with a sense of well-being. It is almost impossible to feel negative when you are laughing and smiling. Regular massages can also help relax your mind and body, as can Mindfulness Based Stress and Anxiety Management Tools.

You can also make changes to your environment that will help you feel better. Put your sensitivity to work by using the space around you as a source of positivity. If you are indoors, let plenty of natural light into the room. Get rid of any clutter, and remove any objects that you find distracting. Cleaning can also be a useful activity. When you clean a room, you are doing something that is both immediately productive and symbolically powerful. As you wash and

---

[29] Orloff, J. (2017). *The Empath's Survival Guide: Life Strategies for Sensitive People.* Sounds True: Boulder, Colorado.

scrub, imagine that you are washing away all the negative thoughts that have been weighing you down. Taking out the trash serves much the same purpose. **Regaining control of your personal space helps you feel more in control of your emotions.** If you can, go and take a short walk outside. Research shows that spending time in nature is soothing.[30] Green spaces and open water are relaxing for empaths. Even a few minutes sitting next to a small pond can make a significant difference.

When you are caught up in a whirl of negative emotions, you can lose sight of the bigger picture. Remind yourself that negative feelings will pass, and that it's unlikely you will even remember these emotions in a few days' time. Put your current feelings into perspective by reminding yourself that you have experienced unpleasant emotional states in the past, but you have survived! What's more, **every time you prove to yourself that you can handle high emotional loads, it shores up your confidence for the future.** Even when you feel somewhat shaky and full of self-doubt, you have the opportunity to reframe the experience as a chance to become stronger and more emotionally resilient.

Psychotherapists sometimes use an exercise known as "Thought Challenging" to help their clients overcome negative beliefs. You can try it for yourself. Take a piece of paper and, at the top, write out your negative beliefs. Next, note down as many pieces of evidence as possible that prove these beliefs wrong. For example, you may want to address negative beliefs you hold regarding your emotional strength. To do this, you would begin by writing down your beliefs, such as "I can't handle tough situations," or "I am a weak person who can't deal with stress." You would then write down reasons why these statements are incorrect. For instance, you could write about the time you handled a stressful project at work, or succeeded in any other endeavor that required emotional strength.

Doing good deeds for others will also help you feel more positive. When you are in a low mood, it feels as though the world is an unkind, unpleasant place. Restore your faith in human nature by doing something for someone else. Ideally, do it in such a way that no-one will ever identify you as the giver. For example, you could give an anonymous donation to charity. Good deeds that allow you to connect with others also work well. You could pay for someone else's drink at a coffee shop, offer to take on some extra work for a stressed colleague, or put in a call to an elderly relative. **You will soon feel better, and someone else benefits**

---

[30] Williams, F. (2017). *This Is Your Brain on Nature.* nationalgeographic.com

too. It's a win-win situation. Why not aim to carry out at least three good deeds per week? Make a note of them in your diary, and look back at your records whenever you hit a slump. **They will serve as concrete proof that there is a lot of good in the world** – people like you are working to make it a better place!

Spending time with a positive person is also an effective way to get rid of negativity. It's true that you might be dragged down by other people's negativity, but you can also benefit from their positive moods too! Phone an upbeat, optimistic friend or relative. You don't need to tell them that you are feeling low. Just ask how they are, let the conversation flow naturally, and enjoy the positive effect they have on your emotional state.

Visualization is another great tool to have on hand for dealing with negative energy. It can be done anywhere, takes only a couple of minutes, and is easy once you find a method that works for you.

Find a calm, quiet place and close your eyes. If you are at work and can't find an empty room, the bathroom will do in a pinch. First, imagine yourself surrounded by a dark cloud of negative energy. Take a few seconds to make this image as vivid as you can. Now re-imagine this picture so that you can "see" a calm, happy, positive version of yourself instead. Imagine the negativity melting away, leaving you feeling calm and relaxed. Make this new mental image as big and as bright as possible. Repeat this visualization several times until this calm, relaxed image is an accurate reflection of your current mental state.

Finally, **gratitude is a wonderful remedy for negativity.** Challenge yourself to list 20 things that you are grateful for in the present moment, from your cup of coffee to the shoes on your feet. **The more thankful you feel, the less of a hold negativity will have over you.** Think of three things you are looking forward to doing in the coming week, such as meeting up with a friend, seeing a movie, or spending a day in the park. Think about how good you will feel when you are doing one of those things. Allow yourself to look forward to this pleasurable activity. Your body will feel increasingly relaxed and comfortable. You will also feel your mood shift, because you will start to see the world as a place of opportunities and happiness. Carrying out random acts of kindness whilst maintaining a grateful attitude is the best recipe for positivity. As an empath, you will naturally feel most comfortable in harmonious environments. However, sometimes you will need to confront negative energy head-on in the form of arguments and confrontations. In the next chapter, I'll show you how to negotiate in tense situations without suffering emotional overload.

Chapter 15: How to Handle Conflict As An Empath

As a rule, empaths do not like conflict. Being so in touch with other people's feelings, the stress that comes with arguments can feel overwhelming. Before I came to accept and work with my empathic nature, I would sometimes have to leave the room in the middle of an argument. Other people would label me "immature" or "rude." In reality, I was neither - the emotional "noise" was just too much for my system to cope with. Unfortunately, I didn't have the confidence or self-awareness to ask those around me if we could take a break. Since then, I have learned a few techniques that help me approach conflict in a healthy way. I'm going to share these with you in this chapter. You will need to modify your attitude towards disagreements, practice your assertiveness, and structure your arguments and negotiations if possible. This may mean that you have to take a critical look at how you currently handle conflict, and how you communicate with others.

Obviously, the easiest way to deal with conflict is to avoid it altogether. This is the coping mechanism favored by many empaths who have yet to learn how to work with their gift. If you are highly sensitive, you may have shied away from developing friendships, or you may even avoid spending time with close relatives in a bid to avoid arguments. This is certainly effective, but it comes at a great price. In avoiding other people, you are denying yourself the opportunity to enjoy the positive side of relationships. **Remember that when you are an empath, other people's joy is your own. Why would you want to miss out on that?** In the long run, it is better to accept that everyone disagrees from time to time. You need to remind yourself that rowing can definitely be stressful, but most of the time there is a resolution at the end. Conflict isn't much fun, but it is rarely fatal. Moreover, if you work on drawing boundaries between yourself and others, there is no reason why arguments should affect you any more than they would affect a non-empath.

Most arguments arise from misunderstandings and breakdowns in communication. Empaths and non-empaths alike are often guilty of expecting others to read our minds. This is impossible, but we tend to think that if our friend or relative really loved us, they would somehow know exactly how we feel and what we want! When we start a romantic relationship with someone, we tend to think that they should be sensitive to our needs at all times. This sets the stage for disappointment, because no-one can truly understand what their partner wants, 24/7. **The solution is clear communication and assertiveness.** Assertive behavior and clear boundaries will prevent most conflicts arising in the first place, because they allow two people to negotiate their own wants and needs before serious misunderstandings have a chance to occur. This is where you can really make the most of your empathic abilities. As you are in touch with how the other person feels, you can sense the beginnings of dissatisfaction before things spiral into conflict. It is better to ask someone why they appear distressed, rather than hope the problem will disappear by itself.

However, some arguments are unavoidable. To help you feel less overwhelmed, learn how to structure discussions so that they stay calm and constructive. **Much of the tension associated with conflict arises when one or both people feel as though their views are being ignored.** Therefore, make sure you allow everyone to state their position and air their feelings. If you are having an argument with someone who is particularly tense or angry, let them take their turn first. This may not feel fair, but **your chances of getting someone to listen when they are in a state of anger and frustration is next to nil.**

Resist the urge to jump in or interrupt them, as this will only make the situation worse. You will find that if you truly give them the space to vent, they will begin to calm down after a few minutes. In the words of communication guru Leil Lowndes, you need to let them "empty their tank."[31]

The next step is to make sure that you have understood what they are saying. You will already have picked up on how they feel, but it is still important to make sure that you appreciate the finer details. You can do this by saying, "Let me see whether I have understood you correctly. You told me that..." Finish the sentence by paraphrasing what they have said. This gives them the opportunity to correct you in case you have misunderstood. Perhaps even more crucially, it will make them feel respected, which in turn puts them in a more receptive frame of mind.

Next, ask for a few minutes in which you can put your own views across. Outline your position in a neutral tone. **Stick to the facts of the situation, and avoid name-calling, blaming, and accusations.** By all means let the other person know how you feel, but do not tell them that they "made" you feel a certain way – this will only make them angrier. Instead, tell them that when they do X, you feel Y. If the other person interrupts you, stop talking and let them

---

[31] Lowndes, L. (2003). How to Talk to Anyone: 92 Little Tricks for Big Success in Relationships. Columbus, OH: McGraw-Hill.

speak. If they are a decent, respectful person, they will not interrupt for long. If they constantly talk over you or become abusive, there is no point trying to have a constructive conversation in the first place. At this point, the best solution is to call a timeout. **Ten or fifteen minutes apart in separate rooms will give you the chance to ground yourself, and allow the other person some time in which to cool off.**

Once you have both had the chance to put forward your perspective, you may need to work together to come up with a solution. Allow plenty of time for this step, because the first one or two solutions you come up with may not be the most effective. If the atmosphere is still tense, you could each write down your ideas in silence for a few minutes before sharing them with one another.

You may find that a bit of creative thinking will generate an answer that works for both of you. In the event of a stalemate, suggest that you get together the next day to continue talking.

If possible, arrange the conversation at a time of day that allows you to take time to "decompress" afterwards. **As an empath, you will need some time to relax and recharge, even if the discussion was relatively calm and productive.** Take a few hours to do something that relaxes you. If a particular friend or relative makes you feel safe and grounded, ask them if you can meet or speak with them after the discussion has finished or the conflict has been resolved. Knowing that you can talk to them later in the day can be enough to boost your confidence.

When you need to discuss and resolve a difficult issue with someone you trust, remind them that you are a highly sensitive person and therefore deeply affected by conflict. Reassure them that you fully intend to engage with them and sort the problem out, but you might need a few accommodations along the way. **It is not a sign of weakness to tell someone what you need – it actually requires a lot of strength to practice this kind of honesty.**

If you cannot find a way to discuss the situation with someone without losing control over your emotions, you can write out your thoughts instead. If you are arguing about a complicated subject or a particularly difficult issue, suggest that you each take an hour to write down how you feel and what the underlying problems might be. For example, if you are arguing with your partner about their tendency to avoid doing their share of the chores, the underlying issue might be their lack of respect for your time and needs. Follow the same guidelines that apply when addressing the problem in person. **Stick to the facts, avoid provocative language, and be clear on what you would like to happen.** Stay in separate rooms as you do this exercise to avoid picking up on the other person's emotions. When you have both had the chance to set down your thoughts in writing, reconvene and swap your pieces of paper. A key advantage of this technique is that both parties can read the statements several times if necessary, and ask for clarification if they don't fully understand what the other is saying.

Make sure you do this exercise in person. E-mails, letters and online messaging services can trigger further misunderstandings, making the situation even worse. Only when all parties are in the same room, and available to clarify what they mean, can you hope to amicably resolve a dispute.

Whilst many empaths never become comfortable with confrontation and conflict, some learn how to overcome their sensitivity to tension and put their empathic nature to good use. Not only can an empath become confident in overcoming problems with other people, but they can also act as effective adjudicator when two or more of their friends or relatives have a disagreement. As long as you can distinguish between your own feelings and those of others, you are likely to be a good mediator. Mediation involves understanding and respecting the opinions and feelings of all parties, so your empathic abilities will help you guide everyone towards a solution that works.

Of course, some people will drag you down and disrupt your emotional equilibrium even during times of peace. In the next chapter, you will learn how to deal with these individuals.

Chapter 16: How to Handle Energy Vampires

Empaths tend to attract all kinds of people. This can be wonderful, and most of us appreciate the opportunity to connect with our fellow humans. Unfortunately, there are certain individuals who not only make life harder for everyone around them, but also have the ability to drain the energy of anyone unlucky enough to cross their path. These people are commonly referred to as "energy vampires." In this chapter, you will learn how to spot various kinds of energy vampire, and learn how to avoid becoming a victim.

According to Judith Orloff, there are several distinct types of energy vampire that an empath needs to watch out for.[32] Each has their own set of characteristics, and requires a particular set of skills if you are to handle them effectively. You should note that not all energy vampires are malicious people. In fact, most of them are completely unaware of the effect they have on others. Nevertheless, for your own psychological health, you should avoid them whenever possible.

Before I go into further detail about the different varieties of energy vampire out there, I'll give you a brief overview of their similarities. Put simply, all energy vampires make you feel mentally and spiritually drained. Unless you are prepared and have a plan in place to deal with them, a few minutes with one of these people is enough to make you feel tired, negative, and even depressed. **If you feel this way on a regular basis after interacting with a certain person, consider the possibility that they may be an energy vampire.**

Let's begin with perhaps the most common type – the Victim. Victims are those people who make your heart sink every time you see them come into a room. When you ask them how their day is going, they never have good news to share. Instead, they give you a rundown of all their latest woes. If nothing has actually gone wrong for them lately, they will talk to you about a gloomy news item they saw on TV, or their personal theories about what is going wrong with the world. Victims are excellent at holding onto grudges, and they put the worst possible spin on every situation. They never pass up the opportunity to tell you how about how other people have screwed them over, why their boss never treats them fairly, why their spouse is a nightmare to live with, and so on.

As a sensitive person who hates the thought of others suffering any kind of emotional pain, your

---

[32] Orloff, J. (2017). *The Empath's Survival Guide: Life Strategies for Sensitive People.* Sounds True: Boulder, Colorado.

first instinct will be to offer support, understanding, and potential solutions. But watch out – a Victim doesn't actually want to be happy. You could offer them the best advice in the world, and listen to them for hours at a time, but they would still complain. **They enjoy playing their role, and they love gaining sympathy from those around them.** You should also be aware that once they have identified someone as a source of sympathy, they will keep on coming back. The more encouragement you give them, the more likely they are to hunt you down in the future. **The solution? Act innocent and don't get caught in the trap of trying to offer them advice – they won't take it.** Instead, acknowledge their suffering with a simple "How awful, I hope things improve soon," and then swiftly change the subject. They might come to the conclusion that you are an unsympathetic person, but this is a much better outcome than adopting the role of their emotional punching bag.

The second type is the Constant Talker. The clue is in the name – these individuals know how to suck the air out of the room. They are not necessarily negative, like the Victim, but they are still draining because they entrap you with story after story. If you have ever been waylaid by a neighbor who can happily talk over the garden fence for an hour at a time, you know exactly what it's like to interact with a Constant Talker. They might ask you a token question here and there, but their main objective is to share as much of their life story with you as possible. They are also often incredibly boring, and tend to repeat the same old stories over and over again. Their primary objective is to get all their thoughts and feelings out in the open, with no concern for other people's time.

Constant Talkers can sometimes be shut down with a simple excuse. Don't wait until you have to think on your feet. Come up with a few plausible excuses in advance that will cover you in any situation. Keep them simple. "I need to make a phone call," "Excuse me, I just need to pop to the restroom," and "Sorry, but I have a deadline I've got to meet," are usually effective.

This strategy isn't subtle, but neither are Constant Talkers! Other people might get the hint if you start yawning from boredom, but Constant Talkers will just keep going, so a firm approach is needed. If you are trapped with a Constant Talker – for example, you are sat next to them at a dinner party – the best tactic is to find some entertainment in what they are saying. Count how many times they say "I," or how many times they repeat themselves. You'll at least enjoy yourself a little.

Then we have Drama Queens. They may not talk for hours on end or believe that the world is against them, but they thrive on drama and chaos. A typical Drama Queen will seize every chance to turn a minor disaster into a crisis. They will have meltdowns at the slightest inconvenience. If someone doesn't return their call or a meeting starts ten minutes late, they will let everyone know how awful they feel. Unfortunately for any empaths nearby, this kind of mental chaos is damaging. You might find that you become caught up in the drama. Their panic can be contagious, and you may find yourself quickly becoming unsettled. Although the name implies that Drama Queens are women, men can display this pattern of behavior too.

Fortunately, a neutral attitude can dampen down their theatrical performance. Do not engage in the drama. Let them whine a little, and then tell them that you trust that they will sort out the problem. Never ask them how they are doing, because they will just rant and whine about their latest melodrama. Move the subject to another topic, or distract them with a task. They tend to respond well to boundaries, and quickly learn when someone isn't going to give them the attention they desperately crave. If you let them have their tantrum whilst remaining completely calm yourself, they will start to feel silly pretty quickly!

You also need to watch out for Control Freaks. These individuals love to impose their opinions on anyone who will listen. Worst of all, they also like to tell others what they should do with their lives. Their favorite phrases include "I think you should…" and "In your position, I would definitely…" However, they don't actually want to help you. **Their agenda is actually to make themselves feel more powerful by attempting to control others.** Control Freaks have little interest in developing meaningful relationships and emotional intimacy, because they are only interested in getting their own way.

You need to be aware that a Control Freak can really wear down your self-confidence, particularly if they are in a position of social or professional power. It is more damaging to hear so-called "helpful suggestions" from a parent or boss than a casual acquaintance. **A Control Freak typically sounds so confident in their opinions that you start to wonder whether you are being shortsighted in refusing to take their advice.** You need to remind yourself that these people do not know you better than you know yourself, and if they truly cared for you, they would offer to listen rather than try to run your life.

Setting your own goals and knowing your own values will help you keep your self-image intact around these people. They will become defensive when you point out that their advice is unsolicited. Phrases such as "I hear what you are saying, I'll bear it in mind" and "That's an interesting perspective" are noncommittal ways of allowing the Control Freak to feel "heard." They will leave the conversation feeling satisfied that they have passed on their wisdom, and you can then go ahead and live your life in a way that suits you.

Finally, we have the Passive Aggressor. This is perhaps the subtlest form of energy vampire. Passive Aggressors are good at putting on a show of politeness, and will say that they have your best interests at heart. However, they often undermine you and make life difficult. For example, a work colleague who claims that they want to "help," yet seems to lose every important document you give them is showing passive-aggressive behavior. Another classic Passive Aggressor tactic is to appear sad or angry, but claim that nothing is wrong if you ask them whether they are OK. This puts everyone else on edge – it's a kind of power trip. They also tend to disguise offensive comments as "jokes." After making a joke at your expense, a Passive Aggressor is likely to accuse you of lacking in humor or being "uptight."

Passive Aggressors need to be called out on their behavior, or else they will assume that they can continue to undermine you with subtle insults. This is especially important if they are belittling you in front of others. Letting them know that you have noticed exactly what they are doing can be enough to trigger change. Questions such as "Joanne, when you said X in front of our coworkers, were you trying to insult me?" make it clear that you an assertive person who isn't afraid to defend your boundaries and emotional health.

However, do not deplete your energy by trying to point out every instance of passive-aggressive behavior. **Pick your battles carefully, and only give a Passive Aggressor one opportunity to change their behavior.** If they don't respond to a neutral, polite request such as "Please do not remove documents from my desk if you are not going to take care of them," the best approach is to avoid trusting them in the future. Lower your expectations and you will save yourself a lot of trouble. If you need to get specific information out of a Passive Aggressor, get their response in writing so that they cannot claim at a later date that you misinterpreted what they were saying.

So, how can you minimize the effects of an energy vampire? Your first weapon is proximity – or rather, a lack thereof. If possible, excuse yourself the minute you realize that you are dealing with a vampire. The probability of getting them to change their behaviors is practically nil. You may try and empathize with them, and wonder what could have happened to them early in life to shape their character in this way. The truth is that it varies on a case-by-case basis. Some energy vampires are truly sociopathic, and show a tendency early in life to manipulate other people. Others have learned to be pessimistic during childhood or adolescence, and their behaviors are mostly down to habit. Others may have experienced trauma or hardships that have colored their worldview.

Whatever the reason, it is not your responsibility to "fix" them.

Energy vampires can only change their ways with deliberate effort and extensive self-reflection. You cannot afford to waste your precious time and energy on someone who probably doesn't even realize that they drag other people down. If you are obliged to spend time with an energy vampire, try the "bookending" technique. Schedule or plan positive, enjoyable activities for the period immediately before and after you are due to spend time with a toxic person.

Energy vampires are one of the biggest threats in your environment. Fortunately, with a little preparation, you can minimize their effects. Even if you end up in a relationship with such a person, you can escape with your psychological and mental health intact. In the next chapter, you will learn how to survive a relationship with a toxic partner.

Chapter 17: How to Handle a Toxic Romantic Relationship

In the previous chapter, you learned how to identify the type of person who will only make your life a misery if you engage with them. However, sometimes we become intimately involved with negative, toxic people anyway. In this chapter, we are going to take a closer look at what you can do if you are already in a relationship with an energy vampire who is sapping your mental and emotional health.

So why might you end up in this kind of relationship? Unfortunately, some toxic people are so good at putting on an act that even an empath can be fooled. **These individuals don't just hide their dark side – they behave in such a way that their victim thinks they have found a like-minded person.** If you have ever been in an abusive relationship with someone you later realized was borderline or even completely sociopathic, you will probably be able to remember the intensity and happiness of the early days. **Someone like this will pretend to be anything you want them to be. They will take on a persona, set of character traits, and even new interests that mirror yours or that they believe will appeal to you.** You feel as though they are a great match for you, and that they might even be "The One." If you have any misgivings, they will be overridden by your partner's sheer charm and apparent sincerity. Unfortunately, **once you are firmly attached and invested in the relationship, the mask comes off.**

Another tactic they might use is to play the wounded victim. A highly sensitive person is keen to help others, and when they come across someone who seems to have problems, they are often moved to pity. Many abusive people know exactly who to target. They seldom admit it aloud, but they know precisely what they are doing, even if they feign innocence. There is nothing wrong in wanting to lend someone moral support, but the trouble starts when romantic feelings enter the picture. **An empath may find themselves caught up in a dramatic relationship whereby they set out to help a "damaged" individual, end up falling in love with them, and then find it almost impossible to detach.**

Narcissists find empaths to be very attractive prospects when searching for a mate, because they know that some will do all they can to help "heal" them. A narcissist sincerely believes that they are superior to others, and that their special status entitles them to preferential treatment. Another defining feature is their apparent lack of empathy. A narcissist may go through the motions of sympathizing with you in times of need, but only as long as you are of use to them. For example, if you have a narcissist working for you, they will be perfectly pleasant as long as they think you are treating them well. However, the moment they are thwarted, the mask soon slips. They can often be angry, scheming, exploitative, and downright abusive. In intimate relationships they frequently have affairs, overlook their partner's emotional needs, and place their desires above those of everyone and anyone else. Their bad behavior stems from a sense of entitlement and poor impulse control. They believe that they are above the law, and do not need to follow the moral codes that govern most people's conduct.

As narcissists frequently lie to get what they want, and as a means of forging superficial connections with others, they tend to make empaths feel uneasy. We are good at identifying liars, and the typical narcissist mix of charisma and deception sets off our radars. If you are a highly sensitive person, you have probably spotted a narcissist well before anyone else in your social circle or team at work figured out what they were up against. They make you feel tense, suspicious, and on edge – in other words, they drain your energy and make your life a misery if you engage with them on a regular basis. Yet at the same time, a high-functioning narcissist might be able to charm their way into your life.

Never allow a narcissist to bowl you over with their energy and charisma. You should also be aware that not all of them appear super-confident. Sometimes, they may pretend to be meek, mild, and just in need of a little help. Once they have snared you in a relationship, they will then begin to manipulate you on a regular basis. It is up to you to trust your intuition. If someone seems too good to be true, think twice before continuing.

Our culture places such a high value on romantic love and finding "someone special," that even when we see red flags, we might march forward in the relationship anyway. We can also fool ourselves into thinking that we can be the one that will make them change their ways. Unfortunately, this seldom works in practice. Yes, it is possible for some toxic people to undertake extensive "inner work," adopt new patterns of behavior, and lose their sense of entitlement. The problem is that this seldom happens as the result of external pressure. Do not waste your time sitting around waiting for them to transform into a better person. Your empathic nature might compel you to help them, but change will only happen when they decide to put in the effort.

If you can't or won't leave a toxic person, you at least need to preserve your emotional health during the relationship. The first step is to find at least one positive outlet that boosts your well-being. **It isn't healthy for anyone to make their partner the center of their universe, but this is doubly true in unhealthy relationships.** As an empath, you will quickly become totally immersed in your partner's toxicity if you don't build a life that includes other people and interests.

You also need to accept that your partner will never be able to meet your need to feel safe and loved. They may be perfectly pleasant some of the time, but all too often they will make you feel down, depressed, and drained. Be realistic and look for other sources for acceptance and love. This kind of love may come in the form of close friends or relatives. If you don't have a support network in place, now is the time to build one. Start small. Join a group relevant to your interests, reconnect with old friends, and work on your family relationships. It's a winning strategy, regardless of what happens between you and your partner. If your romantic relationship improves or at least offers you enough benefits that you stick around, then great. If the situation becomes unbearable, you know that you have people around you who will offer support.

Even if you are dependent on your partner for money or accommodation, you can at least keep your intellectual independence. Take up a hobby that they do not share, and visit places they have no interest in going. Spending time around people who model healthy relationships is also a good idea, because it will help you avoid entering into a state of denial in which you convince yourself that everything is just fine between yourself and your partner. If you don't have an income of your own, take steps towards getting a job or qualification. Cultivate and maintain a positive outlook on life. Build healthy habits, nurture your social life, and consume inspiring media.

Self-confidence is your best defense against toxic people. The more highly you value yourself, the less tolerance you will have for bad behavior in others and the more prepared you will be to defend your boundaries. **Ideally, you'll have your boundaries in place before you start looking for a partner, but it's never too late to assert yourself.** If you notice that someone has been trying to gradually erode your boundaries and treats you in an increasingly disrespectful manner, you need to make a decision. You can stay and hope the relationship gets better by itself (which I would not recommend!), you can leave, or you can stay and try to assert yourself.

In abusive relationships, the abused partner often surrenders their power and loses sight of who they are beyond the confines of the relationship. Let me be absolutely clear on this point – **no-one deserves to be abused, and no-one should believe an abuser who claims otherwise.** My point is that if you are an empath in a toxic relationship, **you do have a choice as to how you handle the situation.**

You may not be able to leave right away, but reaching out to a friend, relative or counselor is still a proactive move. You can choose to start on the path to healing, and reconsider the way in which you choose your partners.

If you are currently single, make sure you equip yourself with the knowledge and tools you need to avoid entering into a toxic relationship in the first place. **It may sound obvious, but avoid dating anyone who makes you feel sorry for them or triggers your "fixer" urges.** They may be a lovely person but, as an empath, you are liable to drown in their negativity and issues. This is not a good foundation for a relationship. By all means get to know them and interact with them as a friend – whilst keeping your boundaries in place, of course – but **do not slip into the role of their savior.**

You'd be forgiven for thinking that the best way of ensuring a happy relationship is to find another empath. However, a pairing of two empaths doesn't necessarily result in a good outcome. In the next chapter, you will discover what you need to look out for when forming friendships and romantic relationships with other empaths.

Chapter 18: Connecting with Other Empaths

One of the most basic human needs is the feeling that comes with being accepted and understood by our family and friends. Unfortunately, empaths are often a mystery to those closest to them. **Connecting with other empaths can give you a sense of community and relief, but you should also be aware of the pitfalls that can arise when two sensitive people form a relationship.** In this chapter, I'll tell you how to form healthy bonds with other empaths. Broadly speaking, the same guidelines apply whether you are looking to form a platonic or romantic relationship.

The most effective way to find other empaths is via the internet. A quick Google search will turn up forums dedicated to empaths and highly sensitive people. There are also a number of active blogs maintained by empaths. People often start conversations in the comments sections of a blog in order to share their experiences. From there, users can swap contact details and develop friendships. In principle, this is a great way to make new friends, but you must be on your guard. First, you need to be aware that not everyone claiming to be an empath actually possesses empathic qualities. The internet is full of misleading information on empathy, empaths, and highly sensitive people. It is easy for the average layperson to become confused about the meaning of these terms, and mistakenly identify themselves as an empath. Tread carefully when you encounter a self-professed empath. It will become apparent quite quickly whether they share your experiences, but proceed with caution. If someone appears misinformed, resist the temptation to point it out. You will only start an argument, and things could quickly turn hostile. It is better to avoid developing the friendship, and instead focus on meeting other people who are able to relate to the typical empath experience. Before engaging with someone, look at their previous posts or blog comments. Do they seem genuine and friendly? Ask yourself whether their stories and feelings resonate with your own.

Unfortunately, there are another group of people you need to watch out for when connecting with other empaths. If you join an online forum geared towards empathic individuals or start commenting on a blog written by an empath, there is a small chance that you will come across people who deliberately target sensitive individuals. They may pose as fellow empaths or people interested in personal development. Unfortunately, they may be looking to take advantage of people who are both caring and vulnerable. It isn't a nice thought, but some sociopaths and narcissists get a thrill from baiting or even abusing others. Do not hesitate to block or report someone who is setting off your inner alarm bells. You are an empath, so trust your intuition. You do not have to justify yourself or "prove" your empathic status to anyone. Neither do you have to tolerate people who just want to play devil's advocate by arguing that empaths and highly sensitive individuals are exactly like everyone else and simply need to "calm down." Let these people waste their own time, and channel your energy into creating meaningful bonds with others.

If you are relieved at having found another likeminded soul, it may take a lot of willpower to ease into a relationship rather than telling them your whole life story within a few days. Remember that both of you are emotional sponges, and digesting a lot of information about a stranger can feel overwhelming. Take your time. Ask light questions at the beginning – how they found the site, how they've been doing lately - and move onto the heavier stuff as you continue your correspondence. The anonymity granted by the internet means that even well-meaning people can become attached far too quickly to strangers who, for all they know, may just be playing a role or out to take advantage of their good nature.

If you develop serious feelings for someone you meet online, try to meet them in person as soon as possible, or at least Skype with them face-to-face. Half an hour of in-person contact will give you a much greater insight into their character than hundreds of online messages.

Meeting other empaths in person rather than online is a safer option for those of us who tend to get attached to the idea of someone we have only met in cyberspace. There aren't many clubs for empaths out there, but sensitive people tend to congregate in places where compassion is valued. **Charities tend to attractive sensitive people, so volunteering for a local organization would be a good place to start.** Depending on your interests and values, you might also wish to join a spiritual or religious group. Sensitive people are often interested in the "big questions" relating to life and the universe, and so you are likely to find a few empaths among religious congregations and spiritual development groups.

A friendship or romantic relationship between two empaths can be truly special. You will both value clear communication, loyalty, and compassion. This is the perfect foundation for a mutually beneficial partnership in which both of you feel supported during tough times. Although neither of you are psychic, at times it will seem as though you can read the mind of your friend or partner. You will become so attuned to one another's mood and body language that a feeling of deep and lasting understanding will flourish.

Sounds wonderful, right? For many empaths, their new friend or partner enriches their life. However, two empaths can become locked in a vicious cycle of codependency. Codependency is a pattern of behavior in which a person comes to rely on someone for their own happiness, and starts to mirror the other person's emotions. Codependents often try and "look after" a friend, relative or partner who is in some way vulnerable. Empaths and highly sensitive people are particularly likely to fall into this trap, as they care too deeply about their friends' and partners' feelings. When you have two empaths in a relationship, both can become overwhelmed by the others' problems. **It's important to spend some time apart, pursue your own interests, and keep your boundaries intact.**

An empath who has felt misunderstood from an early age is likely to become codependent in an attempt to secure the approval of other people. If this sounds like you, it's sensible to work on this issue before seeking close friendships or a romantic relationship. **This is because when you have little idea of who you are beyond the context of your relationships, you are at risk of morphing yourself into whatever the type of character you think another person wants you to be.** Your genuine self gets lost as you act like a chameleon, changing your relationship preferences and even core beliefs in order to secure love and affection. It may work for a while, but eventually you will experience a crisis because you no longer have a solid sense of your own identity.

Be prepared to negotiate plenty of time apart from your empath partner. **Even when you have no particular activity scheduled, both of you will appreciate some alone time on a regular basis once the initial attraction has died down.** You may compare your relationship to that of a "normal" couple, and feel that your partnership is in some way lacking as a result. Remember that most people are not empaths, and so have a higher tolerance for spending prolonged periods of time with their friends and partners. When it comes to relationships, **it's the quality of the time spent together that really counts.** Many empaths believe that it's their alone time that really enables them to bring their best, most understanding selves to the relationship. When they are well-rested and can ground themselves, they are in a better position to process the intense emotions that accompany romantic relationships and intimate friendships.

Do not allow another person to become the center of your life, no matter how well-matched you are. Do not forget about everyone else in your life! Otherwise, should your new relationship come undone, you will be left feeling alone. In addition, keeping up with your relatives and friends can provide you with a reality check if things take an unhealthy turn. For example, if you ask a good friend to tell you whether your romantic relationship is unhealthy, they should be willing to give their honest opinion. You do not have to take their advice, but knowing that you can call on them when you need to share your worries is reassuring.

Both parties in an empath-empath relationship need to take responsibility for their own self-development. Otherwise, they may cause their partners unnecessary suffering. For example, imagine that an empath-empath couple attend a small party held by a mutual friend. Unfortunately, they are cornered by an energy vampire who won't stop talking and offering them unsolicited "advice." If one partner fails to take a proactive approach in discouraging this individual and merely stands there listening in a passive fashion, both members of the couple might be drawn into a draining conversation that prevents them enjoying the event. **Both must learn how to handle their own emotions, and how to navigate social situations. If one party relies too much on the other, this could lead to feelings of resentment.**

Empaths can find it hard to detach from others, especially if they worry about how their friend or partner will handle the end of the relationship. There may be considerable pain on both sides, and fear of this emotional distress can be enough to keep people in relationships that should have ended long ago. Some people, especially women, were taught as children and young people that "true love" means never giving up on a relationship, even if it is damaging. However, male empaths can also show unhealthy levels of attachment and codependency. Remember that true love will always feel nourishing. It does not leave you feeling drained or depleted. If your relationship does not improve despite your best efforts, it's time to walk away. Counseling and talking about your problems may work in some situations, but be realistic – sometimes you have to cut your losses and move on. Some people cannot or will not change, and building a happy relationship with a healthy individual is a much better use of your time than trying to force a bad relationship to work.

Chapter 19: Masculine, Feminine, or Both?

Empathy is traditionally associated with femininity, but empaths can be male or female. Popular stereotypes surrounding men, women and empathy can be damaging to all sensitive people. For example, female empaths are sometimes dismissed as "too emotional," and male empaths may be labeled "effeminate." In other words, they may be mocked for showing traits more commonly attributed to women. In this chapter, I want to highlight the particular challenges faced by empaths of both sexes, and how these can be overcome. You can learn to embrace both the masculine and feminine parts of your personality. In fact, **I would argue that the healthiest individuals – whether they are empaths or not – are those who are comfortable in behaving either "like a man" or "like a woman", depending on a situation.**

The question of natural differences between the sexes has been a point of contention for literally thousands of years. Whatever your position, you will be able to find sources to support it. For example, some psychologists believe that almost all sex differences are down to socialization, whereas others believe that men and women are so dissimilar from birth that they might as well be different species. I'm going to put forward a radical idea and say that ultimately, **it doesn't really matter exactly how similar we are, or what the causes of these differences might be.** All we need to know for the purposes of this book is that the two sexes experience the world in unique ways. Socialization certainly plays a role here, but there are also underlying biological differences at work. For example, men and women each have distinct hormone profiles, and this goes some way in explaining why the sexes exhibit different behavioral and emotional responses. Whether sex differences are due to nature, nurture or a combination of both, **what's more important is that every empath learns to balance all aspects of their personality.**

We'll start by looking at problems unique to empathic men. There are no reliable statistics that can tell us how many empaths are male, but I'm willing to bet there are more out there than most people would believe. As an empathic man, this topic is of great interest to me! I can tell you from personal experience that most men have never been encouraged to express their innermost thoughts, or even to bother finding out how other people are feeling. This means that sensitive boys learn, from a young age, to avoid talking about emotions in general. It is socially acceptable for males to express anger and jealousy, but not sadness, anxiety, grief, or compassion. Sensitive men can therefore feel isolated. They often wonder why they can't just hide their true feelings like most of their peers.

I like to think that I am an open-minded person, but when my therapist suggested I might be an empath, I felt uncomfortable. When I was a young boy, my parents would tell me to "stop crying like a girl" if I got upset. This taught me that showing feminine qualities made me some kind of failure, so I learned to suppress them. It took a lot of self-reflection to realize that being in touch with my feminine side is actually an advantage, and that I needed to accept who I was in order to be a well-adjusted empath. If you are a male empath, I'd encourage you to think critically about the messages you received whilst growing up. What did your family, friends, teachers and the media tell you?

You can choose to examine these beliefs, and then reject them if they no longer serve a purpose. Beliefs that helped you survive during childhood might be harming you as an adult. Sometimes, children use maladaptive coping mechanisms to help them cope with stressful or abusive environments. Unfortunately, these mechanisms set them up for relationship problems later in life. For example, if you were taught that boys should not cry or tell others when they are feeling low, you are unlikely to feel confident in telling friends and relatives how you feel once you reach adulthood. If you are an empath, you then face an additional problem – you will be deeply affected by other people's emotions, and yet be unable to talk about it.

Connecting with other empathic men is an excellent way to build self-acceptance. Being able to discuss gender roles and the problems that come with being an emotionally open man will help you embrace your gift. Online empathic communities may be dominated by women, but there are men there too if you look closely! Remember that just because you possess stereotypically feminine traits, you are no less of a man. Men can be strong, independent, competitive – and compassionate, empathic and caring too. Yes, some men and women are only comfortable around men who conform to the "strong and silent" mold, but both sexes are drawn to male empaths. If you are looking for a female partner, it may reassure you to know that a lot of women admire men who are able to talk about their feelings. Empathic, sensitive men make loving partners and excellent parents.

Think carefully about the people in your social circle. Are they relatively open-minded about gender roles, or are they quick to insult any man who seems too "girly"? This is actually a form of sexism, as this attitude implies that being like a girl or woman is intrinsically bad. When you truly see men and women as equals, "girly" or "effeminate" are no longer insults – just ignorant and bigoted comments by insecure people. Seek out those who are willing to acknowledge that anyone can possess any number of personality traits, and that there is nothing wrong with that.

What about women? In Western cultures, it is considered far more acceptable to express your emotions if you happen to be a woman. Feminine qualities such as compassion and empathy are perceived as normal and natural in women, but undesirable in men. People tend to assume that women are innately more emotional compared to men, and so they are more likely to accept a woman as an empath. The very fact that "women's intuition" is a popular phrase shows that society upholds the idea that women tend to "just know" things that sail over the heads of men. However, a female empath who gets a gut feeling about a particular person or situation may be dismissed as just a neurotic woman. Despite the advances women have made in science, math and other so-called "masculine" subjects, they are still stereotyped as irrational. **This means that they may hold back from sharing their thoughts and feelings, especially if they are trying to gain credibility in a male-dominated environment.** One coping strategy women sometimes use is to act like "one of the boys." This can work in securing acceptance from male friends and colleagues. However, in doing this, an empathic woman is going against her true nature. She is putting on an act in order to get positive attention, and over time, this will eat away at her self-esteem.

Women often struggle to assertive themselves when defending their boundaries.[33] As you know, empaths can only function properly in relationships once they have learned to uphold their boundaries and assert themselves. These are challenging skills for many empaths, but women frequently experience difficulties in maintaining an appropriate distance between themselves and others. Girls are socialized to be "caring" and "nice," even at the expense of their own autonomy. They are encouraged to play with dolls, and to role-play characters who are both pretty and compliant, the typical example being Disney-type princesses.[34] This type of socialization means that a woman who knows she would be better off abandoning a toxic relationship, or asking someone to stop violating her boundaries, might feel uneasy when she

---

[33] De Azvedo Hanks, J., & Eisler, R. (2016). *The Assertiveness Guide for Women: How To Communicate Your Needs, Set Healthy Boundaries & Transform Your Relationships.* Oakland, CA: New Harbinger Books
[34] Fine, C. (2011). *Delusions of Gender.* New York, NY: Norton & Company

goes against norms dictating "proper" feminine behavior.

The only way for an empathic woman to empower herself is to work on creating and upholding a strong sense of identity and self-esteem. **In much the same way that a male empath benefits from talking to other sensitive men, empathic women gain a lot from connecting with empathic but strong women, who have learned to balance their feminine traits with the assertive, masculine part of their personalities.**

Whilst there are definitely common problems that are specific to each sex, male and female empaths have more similarities than differences. We are all sensitive to other people's emotions, we are all deeply moved by suffering, and we all have to strike that balance between forming bonds with others whilst honoring our need for plenty of personal space. An empath can tune into another person's emotional frequency, whatever gender either party happens to be. Empaths feel on a deep level that every human being is part of something greater. This phenomenon is known as "oneness," and recognizing this truth on a deep level can be the foundation of a spiritual experience.

Most empaths have to undergo a grueling personal journey before they can truly accept their gifts. **To help you make sense of what has happened in your past, you need to learn how to process your memories and look to the future.** In the next chapter, I'll show you how to do just that.

Chapter 20: Letting Go & Coming to Terms With The Past

Everyone holds onto the past too tightly at times, but this behavior can be particularly devastating for empaths. In this chapter, you will discover why empaths often feel a great deal of pain and regret about their pasts, and how this will continue to affect their behavior if left unaddressed. You will also learn the tools and techniques you need in order to come to terms with what has happened, forgive others, and adopt a more positive outlook in the future.

So why do empaths typically have more than their fair share of regrets? **The primary reason is our memory for emotional experiences.** I can still remember the agony of being turned down by my first crush, the time I embarrassed myself in a supermarket when my card got declined three times in a row, and the feeling of being hauled before my first boss for a disciplinary meeting. Sure, everyone has bad memories, but for an empath, even the small stuff can become overwhelming if you give it sufficient breathing room. In just a few seconds, everything can come flooding back. **That's why we need to learn how to let go of what has already happened. Only then can we come to terms with the past.**

The examples I gave above are relatively minor. What about the bigger stuff – childhood abuse, traumatic breakups, serious illnesses, and so forth? The same basic principles apply, except that these incidents are more likely to wreak havoc on your emotional health over the long term. In some cases, you may walk around with residual feelings that have left marks on your psyche. For example, if a long-term partner suddenly broke up with you, this might leave you feeling fundamentally unlovable. This isn't a good foundation for a future relationship. You may find yourself falling into the same old patterns again and again, looking for love and attention in all the wrong places!

Another reason why empaths often have troubled relationships with the past is because so many of us were misunderstood as children and teenagers. Once I realized that my parents' tendency to label me as "too sensitive" or "overly emotional" had really knocked my self-esteem as a young adult, I became angry. I reasoned that if they had been more understanding, I would have enjoyed a happier childhood and a more balanced adolescence. I had to work through this anger and resentment before I could build a healthier relationship with my parents.

So how can you let go? According to psychologist John Grohol,[35] there are five steps you need to take before you can move forward. The first step may sound strange, but it is essential. In brief, you must decide to let go of the pain. At this point, you may be thinking, "Of course I want to let go of the pain! Why would I cling to it?" **Unfortunately, sometimes there is a payoff for holding onto pain. It gives you a feeling of self-righteousness that can feel empowering.** You might also try and influence other people's feelings by playing the martyr. Worse, your pain may have come to define you. If you allow this to happen, you risk turning into a Victim-type emotional vampire. That's a chilling thought, isn't it? If you have held on to a specific grudge or grievance for a long time, be honest with yourself. **What's the payoff for you**? Is it just a habit by this point, or are you using your pain to protect yourself? Only once you have gained insight into your own behavior can you move forward.

The second step is to give yourself time and space to express your feelings. This is not the same as wallowing in your emotions, or indulging in self-pity. Vent your feelings in a journal, talk to a counselor for a few hours, or ask a friend if you can talk to them over a coffee. Again, the objective is not to remain stuck in your pain, but to **express it.** At this point, you should assess whether you played any part in the situation, and what you can learn from it. For example, your ex-partner may have once cheated on you, but you may have refused to talk to them when they tried to tell you that they were unhappy in the relationship. In future, you might make a special effort to improve your communication skills.

Once you have unburdened yourself, **make the decision to take responsibility for your own feelings.** Yes, another person may have behaved badly, but how you respond is now up to you. You can choose to adopt a victim role, or you can start thinking about how to make your life more joyful. Filling your life with positive experiences in the here and now can be very healing. I'm not saying that living in the present moment is easy, especially if you have fallen into the habit of ruminating on the same memories day after day, but you need to address this pattern if you are to move on. **Create a short, meaningful mantra that will bring you back to the present whenever you begin to dwell on past hurts.** Something like "That was then, this is now," or "I choose to live in the present, and with joy," can work well.

As you become less defined by your pain, you will begin to think about the source of your hurt on a less frequent basis. You will notice that your interactions with other people become happier,

---

[35] Grohol, J. (2014). Learning to Let Go of Past Hurts: 5 Ways to Move On psychcentral.com

and that you are less affected by negative behavior. This is great news for a highly sensitive person, because it means you will be less likely to hold on to other grudges and hurts in the future.

In order to truly move on from the past, you will need to forgive those who have wronged you. For obvious reasons, this can be difficult. When you think about what it would be like to forgive someone, you might feel as though you are letting them get away with what they did. **However, the truth is that your feelings make little difference to them, so you may as well move on anyway!** For example, let's say that your ex-girlfriend cheated on you two years ago before moving away to start a new life with someone else, and you still feel angry and bitter as a result. **By holding onto your anger, the only person you are hurting is yourself.** Your ex-girlfriend is going to carry on living her life whether or not you forgive her. It is pointless to hold yourself back by dwelling on what has happened in the past.

Remember too that forgiving someone is not the same thing as approving of their actions. You can feel neutral or even positive feelings toward someone who has done something wrong, without actually condoning their behavior. Parents are often good at this. If you have children, you will have chosen to forgive bad behavior whilst still feeling a great deal of love toward them. At the same time, there is no need to keep a toxic person in your life if they have hurt you. Don't become a martyr or doormat. **Forgiveness is a personal decision to move on from what happened, regardless of whether the person or people involved deserve to remain in your life.**

Making something good come from your past pain is another potential path to healing. For example, if you were abused by a former partner, you could consider fundraising for a charity that helps victims of domestic violence. You cannot undo the past, but you can at least bring something positive from your experience. Take an inventory of what your past has taught you about yourself and the world. Of course, you would rather have never suffered any losses or failures, but you can channel your negative emotions in a constructive manner. Over time, you might even start to feel thankful that you experienced various problems and setbacks.

Processing your experiences will also help you become a more sensitive, understanding, and less judgmental person. As an empath, you are already more caring than the average person, but you can still use your experiences as a springboard for developing even greater connections with others. You will be able to relate to people not only because you can tap into their feelings, but also because you have walked in their shoes. As long as you have moved past your original feelings of hurt, even your worst memories can help to build bridges between yourself and other people.

Finally, you can also use your past suffering as the basis for creative expression and development. Many great works of art have been fueled by emotion, so think about the ways in which you could channel your pain into writing, music, visual art, or performing. **Art can help you find closure.** For example, if you write a story or novel based on a notable episode in your life, you get to decide on a different ending. You can even make up a fictional epilogue that brings together loose threads. Sometimes, sharing your art with other people can be helpful. It is rewarding to create something that entertains others, and positive critical reception is a good self-esteem boost. On the other hand, if you are sensitive to criticism, it is sometimes best to keep your work private.

Chapter 21: Staying in Harmony With Your Environment

This chapter is about the practical steps you can take to create a soothing environment, wherever you happen to be. As a highly sensitive person, your quality of life will improve once you learn how to minimize the effects of other people's emotions on your psychological state. **However, your physical environment is also key to emotional balance.** In this chapter, I'll offer you some practical suggestions for creating spaces that soothe your sensitive nature.

Let's start with the basics. Most empaths find clutter to be unbearable, because it is too stimulating. When you think about it, it's just common sense. If you have a plethora of ornaments, old magazines or other unnecessary junk lying around then you will be annoyed by the mess every single time you come into the room. This isn't conducive to good emotional health. You might think that tidying up won't make much of a difference, but I promise you that a neat living space will help you feel much calmer. Your home should be a sanctuary, a place you can retreat to when the noise and bustle of the outside world feels overpowering. It will be easier to move past stress and negativity if your personal space fosters positivity.

If you have access to a garden, make the most of it. You do not have to be an expert to enjoy the benefits that come with tending flowers, vegetables, fruit, or whatever else you feel like growing. **Being in nature gives us a sense of perspective. It teaches us that whatever happens, the world keeps turning.** The seasons keep on changing, plants keep growing, and there is always something beautiful to see if you make the effort to look. Gardening is good exercise, relieves stress, and helps maintain emotional equilibrium. If you do not have a garden, why not consider a window box, make a terrarium, or perhaps set up an aquarium?

Sensitive people react strongly to specific kinds of lighting, so consider whether the light sources in your home and workplace help or hinder your emotional state. Fluorescent strip lighting is likely to cause you headaches, and flickering lights will probably make you feel irritable. Replace them with softer lighting that will not trigger sensory overload. Rather than using bright white bulbs, try replacing them with models that emit a soft yellow glow. If you are easily woken every sunrise, buy some blackout curtains. If the buzz or ring of your alarm clock startles you every morning, invest in a light-based clock instead. These gradually emit light in a way that imitates a natural sunrise. The idea is that you wake up naturally, feeling calm and ready to face the day ahead.

Color can also play a role in how you feel. This has been established for thousands of years. Ancient Egyptian physicians used color therapy to help people regain emotional balance, and this holistic practice (known as "chromotherapy") continues today. **Everyone has their own preferences, but particular colors tend to elicit certain feelings, and even spur us to take action.**[36] For example, white is often associated with cleanliness, purity, and the potential for a fresh start. For an empath, it might be the perfect choice when creating a living room that encourages relaxation after a busy day. However, some people find white too sterile and intimidating. They are likely to prefer a soft cream or yellow instead.

Red conveys action and drama, so may be too stimulating for a highly sensitive individual. The color blue is an interesting case. It is often associated with stability and reliability, inducing a sense of calm. At the same time, it is also linked with enhanced productivity. Think about how color affects you when you next decorate your home. There is no right or wrong answer – color preferences and associations are shaped partly by culture and experience, so don't be surprised if your choices differ from those of your friends and other empaths. For example, the color white is associated with death and mourning in some Eastern cultures. If you have been raised in a Western tradition, this may seem like an alien concept!

You probably can't ask your boss to change the décor at work, but you can still adapt the environment in subtle ways that help you maintain a positive frame of mind. A blanket or cushion in your favorite color can boost your mood, so place one on your chair. A small pot plant can help you feel calmer and more in touch with nature, even if you work in a sterile office environment. If there is too much clutter lying around the office, volunteer to sort it out. It might not seem fair if tidying isn't in your job description, but a neat workspace will help you remain calm and productive.

These tips all work as long as you have the ability to make changes in your environment. Unfortunately, most of us have to spend a lot of time in places that other people have designed, and most of these designers will not have created rooms or buildings with empaths in mind. You may also work for a controlling boss who doesn't take kindly to even small changes. This is where grounding objects can be useful. **A grounding object is any item that makes you feel safe and secure.** It could be a key ring, a stone, or piece of jewelry. It doesn't really matter

---

[36] Cherry, K. (2017). *Color Psychology: Does It Affect How You Feel?* verywell.com

what the object is, as long as it is portable and holds positive associations for you.

When you are in an environment that makes you uncomfortable, touch or hold your grounding object. **As you do so, think about the associations you have with this item.** If you know that you are going to spend time in a hostile environment for a few hours, you may also choose to wear a piece of clothing that holds special memories for you. Some highly sensitive people find the sensation of pressure to be soothing. When you remove a jacket or sweater, discreetly place it in your lap rather than on the back of a chair.

You will also need to regulate the type and level of noise in your surroundings. Even day-to-day noises such as wind chimes in a neighbor's garden, or the sound of a colleague typing on a keyboard, can be enough to trigger a minor meltdown for a highly sensitive person. When it comes to unpleasant and distracting noises, you have two options. The first is to tackle the source of the noise directly, but this may not always be possible. For example, it isn't reasonable to ask other people in the office to stop doing their jobs!

The second strategy, which is effective in almost all situations, is to drown out irritating noises with sounds that help you calm down. Natural sounds such as recordings of waves against rocks are excellent tools for lowering your stress levels and keeping you focused. For instance, you could try this website/application: https://www.noisli.com/. When I used to work in an office, I would play these kinds of recordings through a large pair of headphones whenever my colleagues started gossiping in the cubicle next door. I could have asked them to be quiet, but I had learned from past experience that they would only have started again a few minutes later! Headphones also discourage other people from bothering you with trivial tasks and questions, so they are a good defense against irritating people and energy vampires. I have also found binaural beats and white/pink noise to be extremely helpful. You can find hundreds of different playlists on YouTube.

Scents are another factor to consider when making your home or workplace empath-friendly. Many of us find perfume, aftershave, and even some types of deodorant to be overwhelming. We can also tell when someone has changed the air freshener in a room or car. Empaths often suffer chemical sensitivities and allergies, so these products and substances can be highly irritating. Strong scents can also trigger headaches in a sensitive person. Stick to plain and organic cosmetics whenever possible. Place fresh flowers in a room or light candles made with natural ingredients or use natural essential oils and diffusers as a substitute for commercial air fresheners. If you have friends who like to wear strong fragrances, ask them whether they would mind reducing the amount they apply when they know the two of you will be spending time together. This request may seem a little eccentric, but a true friend will understand and respect your needs.

Finally, be aware of images in your environment. As an empath, you are highly affected by violent, graphic or upsetting pictures. Think carefully before hanging a morose painting or photograph in your home, because it has the potential to bring down your mood on a recurring basis. Choose uplifting artwork instead. If you read a newspaper or magazine that features sensationalist headlines on the front page or cover, tuck it away when you are not reading it. Keeping up with current affairs is all well and good if you really need to do so, but consider the effect that reading gloomy news stories has on your state of mind. **Make time to watch or read some positive media too.** Personally, I try to avoid news as much as possible and I do not even have a TV service at home. **Should something important happen, I came to a realization that I would certainly get to know about it from relatives, friends, family and social media.** There is no need to stay tuned to the latest drama from all around the world 24/7, especially when it is so often biased and dramatized by the media.

Despite your sensitivities, you can learn to live in harmony with your environment. It just takes a little creativity, and a few careful adjustments.

Chapter 22: Conclusion - How to Make The World A Better Place With Your Gift

In this final chapter, you will learn how to further develop yourself as an empath. By now, you will appreciate how much sensitive people have to offer the world. I'm going to give you a few suggestions for making the most of your gifts, whatever your age and background. **You have the potential to make an enormous difference at both a local and global level, so why not make your self-development a key focus in your life?**

I'll start by talking about the most local level of all – the family environment. Empaths often improve the emotional health of their relatives, and leave a positive legacy for future generations. A classic example is the empath who breaks a family pattern of abuse or indifference. It is common for abusive individuals to have been abused themselves as children. **The result is a set of negative patterns and addictions that are passed on from generation to generation.** When an empath is born into such a family, they quickly and intuitively appreciate how harmful these unhealthy behaviors are. At a minimum, they will avoid modeling the same patterns to their own children. At best, they will be able to help their relatives learn a more open, gentler style of communication. It is not your job to "fix" your family, but by choosing a more constructive parenting style when raising your own children, you will leave the world a better place.

If you come from an unhealthy family, learn to defend your boundaries and remember that your emotional style will always be different to that of your relatives. You may come under attack for being too "soft" with your children, but trust your intuition and they will turn out just fine.

Going beyond the immediate family environment, an empowered, self-aware empath can lighten the mood in almost any situation. Most people are attracted to, and inspired by, compassion. As empaths, we can act as a positive influence for everyone we come across. As long as you learn how to manage your emotions and handle negative people, you have the power to make almost anyone feel happier just by interacting with them.

You know those people who lift the entire room the moment they walk in? **Those people are often empaths who have learned how to handle their heightened sensitivity. With enough time and skill, there is no reason why you cannot join their ranks.**

You will also come across empaths who are not aware of their gift, or who are aware of their empathic nature but have not received the guidance they need in order to make the most of it.

Stand up for these individuals, and lend them your support whenever possible. If others mock them for being overly sensitive, champion diversity and point out that the world needs empathic people. You may even find that you become an informal mentor to an undeveloped empath. Helping someone come to terms with their status as an empath is rewarding. It allows you to pass on strategies that have enabled you to live in harmony with other people's emotions, and in the world at large. **Encourage them to work on setting boundaries, distinguishing between their emotions and those of other people, and ridding themselves of negative energy.**

If you have the opportunity to pursue a leadership role – whether in a professional or voluntary capacity – then take it. Businesses, charities and governments need leaders who can do more than put together a company strategy and issue orders. **It is becoming increasingly clear that we need leaders who truly care about their workforce, their clients, and the environment**. As a leader, you can influence many people for the better, and this positivity will spread. You don't need to become the CEO of a giant corporation – acting as a leader for a local charity group is also a great way to use your empathic powers for the greater good.

Perhaps the most obvious way of sharing your abilities is to choose a career that demands a high level of empathic skill, but taking short courses is another way of making the most of your strengths without having to expose yourself to all the requirements and responsibilities that come with a particular career. For example, you might not want to become a therapist, but taking a part-time counseling skills course one evening per week would allow you to make good use of your gift. If you do want to make your empathic talents the basis of your career, look beyond the obvious "empath jobs" such as nursing and teaching. Your unusual sensitivity can be put to work in interior design, risk management, or any role that requires you to consider the needs of others.

You should anticipate that your needs and strengths will change over time. In order to function successfully as an empath, **you should respect the fact that you will probably need to adjust your approach to socializing at various points in your life.** During their teens and early twenties, empaths often struggle to find their place in society. They feel different to their peers, and at this age seek acceptance above all else. Fortunately, most come to realize that they have been blessed with a special gift. They begin to relax, knowing that they have a valuable part to play in making the world a better place. At this point, they allow themselves to truly get in touch with their emotions. Often, this allows them to build strong friendships. By the time an empath reaches middle age, they will have a repertoire of techniques and strategies that work for them, and will also have become more accomplished in the art of self-acceptance. At the same time, some older empaths become increasingly intolerant of people who annoy or drain them. They need to find a balance between self-protection and placing themselves at risk of social isolation.

Whatever age you happen to be, don't forget to put yourself first. Empaths often concern themselves with other people's problems and feelings to the detriment of their own well-being. If this sounds familiar, **remember that you are not much use to other people if you are feeling physically or psychologically unwell.**

Put in place a self-care routine that helps you feel strong and grounded. Don't make the mistake of waiting until you hit a crisis before learning how to take care of yourself. **Do at least one activity or conscious practice every day that helps you stay positive, balanced, and in tune with your own feelings.** Both you and those around you will thank you for it! I wish you all the best as you journey along your path to becoming an empowered, happy empath! Good luck! <u>**One last thing before you go – Can I ask you a favor? I need your help!**</u> **If you like this book, could you please share your experience here on Amazon (<u>http://tinyurl.com/reviewmyempathbook</u>) and write an honest review?**

It will be just one minute for you (I will be happy even with one sentence!), but a GREAT help for me and definitely good Karma ☺. Since I'm not a well-established author and I don't have powerful people and big publishing companies supporting me, <u>I read every single review and jump around with joy like a little kid every time my readers comment on my books and give me their honest feedback!</u> If I was able to inspire you in any way, please let me know! It will also help me get my books in front of more people looking for new ideas and useful knowledge.

If you did not enjoy the book or had a problem with it, please don't hesitate to contact me at <u>contact@mindfulnessforsuccess.com</u> **and tell me how I can improve it to provide more value and more knowledge to my readers.** I'm constantly working on my books to make them better and more helpful.

Thank you and good luck! I believe in you and I wish you all the best on your new journey!
Your friend,
Ian

My Free Gift to You – <u>Get One of My Audiobooks For Free!</u>

If you've never created an account on Audible (the biggest audiobook store in the world), **you can claim one free audiobook of mine**!
It's a simple process:
1. Pick one of my audiobooks on Audible:
http://www.audible.com/search?advsearchKeywords=Ian+Tuhovsky
Shortened link: http://tinyurl.com/IanTuhovskyAudiobooks

2. Once you choose a book and open its detail page, click the orange button "Free with 30-Day Trial Membership."
3. Follow the instructions to create your account and download your first free audiobook. Note that you are NOT obligated to continue after your free trial expires. You can cancel your free trial easily anytime, and you won't be charged at all.

Also, if you haven't downloaded your free book already:

Discover How to Get Rid of Stress & Anxiety and Reach Inner Peace in 20 Days or Less!

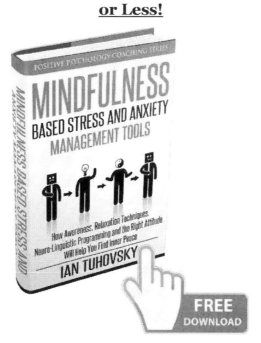

To help speed up your personal transformation, I have prepared a special gift for you!
Download my full, 120 page e-book "Mindfulness Based Stress and Anxiety

Management Tools" for free by clicking here.

Link:

tinyurl.com/mindfulnessgift

Hey there like-minded friends, let's get connected!

Don't hesitate to visit:
-My Blog: www.mindfulnessforsuccess.com
-My Facebook fanpage: https://www.facebook.com/mindfulnessforsuccess
-My Instagram profile: https://instagram.com/mindfulnessforsuccess
-My Amazon profile: amazon.com/author/iantuhovsky

Recommended Reading for You:

If you are interested in Self-Development, Psychology, Social Dynamics, PR, Soft Skills, Spirituality and related topics, you might be interested in previewing or downloading my other books:

Emotional Intelligence Training: A Practical Guide to Making Friends with Your Emotions and Raising Your EQ

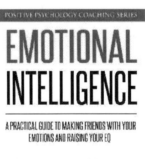

Do you believe your life would be healthier, happier and even better, if you had more practical strategies to regulate your own emotions?
Most people would say yes.
Or, more importantly:
Do you believe you'd be healthier and happier if everyone who you live with had the strategies to regulate their emotions?

...Right?

The truth is not too many people actually realize what EQ is really all about and what causes its popularity to grow constantly.

Scientific research conducted by many American and European universities prove that the **"common" intelligence responses account for less than 20% of our life achievements and successes, while the other over 80% depends on emotional intelligence.** To put it roughly: **either you are emotionally intelligent, or you're doomed to mediocrity, at best.**

As opposed to the popular image, emotionally intelligent people are not the ones who react impulsively and spontaneously, or who act lively and fiery in all types of social environments. Emotionally intelligent people are open to new experiences, can show feelings adequate to the situation, either good or bad, and find it easy to socialize with other people and establish new contacts. They handle stress well, say "no" easily, realistically assess the achievements of themselves or others and are not afraid of constructive criticism and taking calculated risks. **They are the people of success.** Unfortunately, this perfect model of an emotionally intelligent person is extremely rare in our modern times.

Sadly, nowadays, **the amount of emotional problems in the world is increasing at an alarming rate.** We are getting richer, but less and less happy. Depression, suicide, relationship breakdowns, loneliness of choice, fear of closeness, addictions—this is clear evidence that we are getting increasingly worse when it comes to dealing with our emotions. **Emotional intelligence is a SKILL, and can be learned through constant practice and training, just like riding a bike or swimming!**

This book is stuffed with lots of effective exercises, helpful info and practical ideas. Every chapter covers different areas of emotional intelligence and shows you, **step by step**, what exactly you can do to **develop your EQ** and become the **better version of yourself**.
I will show you how freeing yourself from the domination of left-sided brain thinking can contribute to your inner transformation—**the emotional revolution that will help you redefine who you are and what you really want from life!**

<u>**In This Book I'll Show You:**</u>

• What Is Emotional Intelligence and What Does EQ Consist of?
• How to **Observe and Express** Your Emotions
• How to **Release Negative Emotions** and **Empower the Positive Ones**
• How to Deal with Your **Internal Dialogues**
• How to **Deal with the Past**
• **How to Forgive** Yourself and How to Forgive Others
• How to Free Yourself from **Other People's Opinions and Judgments**
• What Are "Submodalities" and How Exactly You Can Use Them to **Empower Yourself** and **Get Rid of Stress**
• The Nine Things You Need to **Stop Doing to Yourself**
• How to Examine Your Thoughts
• **Internal Conflicts** Troubleshooting Technique
• The Lost Art of Asking Yourself the Right Questions and **Discovering Your True Self!**

• How to Create Rich Visualizations
• LOTS of practical exercises from the mighty arsenal of psychology, family therapy, NLP etc.
• **And many, many more!**

Direct Buy Link to Amazon Kindle Store:
https://tinyurl.com/IanEQTrainingKindle
Paperback version on Createspace: https://tinyurl.com/ianEQpaperback

Communication Skills Training: A Practical Guide to Improving Your Social Intelligence, Presentation, Persuasion and Public Speaking

Do You Know How To Communicate With People Effectively, Avoid Conflicts and Get What You Want From Life?

...It's not only about what you say, but also about WHEN, WHY and HOW you say it.

Do The Things You Usually Say Help You, Or Maybe Hold You Back?

Have you ever considered **how many times you intuitively felt that maybe you lost something important or crucial, simply because you unwittingly said or did something, which put somebody off?** Maybe it was a misfortunate word, bad formulation, inappropriate joke, forgotten name, huge misinterpretation, awkward conversation or a strange tone of your voice?
Maybe you assumed that you knew exactly what a particular concept meant for another person and you stopped asking questions?
Maybe you could not listen carefully or could not stay silent for a moment? **How many times have you wanted to achieve something, negotiate better terms, or ask for a**

promotion and failed miserably?

It's time to put that to an end with the help of this book.

Lack of communication skills is exactly what ruins most peoples' lives.
If you don't know how to communicate properly, you are going to have problems both in your intimate and family relationships.

You are going to be ineffective in work and business situations. It's going to be troublesome managing employees or getting what you want from your boss or your clients on a daily basis. Overall, **effective communication is like an engine oil which makes your life run smoothly, getting you wherever you want to be.** There are very few areas in life in which you can succeed in the long run without this crucial skill.

What Will You Learn With This Book?

-What Are The **Most Common Communication Obstacles** Between People And How To Avoid Them
-How To Express Anger And Avoid Conflicts
-What Are **The Most 8 Important Questions You Should Ask Yourself** If You Want To Be An Effective Communicator?
-**5 Most Basic and Crucial** Conversational Fixes
-How To Deal With Difficult and Toxic People
-Phrases to **Purge from Your Dictionary** (And What to Substitute Them With)
-The Subtle Art of **Giving and Receiving Feedback**
-Rapport, the **Art of Excellent Communication**
-How to Use Metaphors to **Communicate Better** And **Connect With People**
-What Metaprograms and Meta Models Are and How Exactly To Make Use of Them To **Become A Polished Communicator**
-How To Read Faces and **How to Effectively Predict Future Behaviors**
-How to Finally Start **Remembering Names**
-How to Have a Great Public Presentation
-How To Create Your Own **Unique Personality** in Business (and Everyday Life)
-Effective Networking

Direct link to Amazon Kindle Store: https://tinyurl.com/IanCommSkillsKindle

Paperback version on Createspace:

http://tinyurl.com/iancommunicationpaperback

Self-Discipline: Mental Toughness Mindset: Increase Your Grit and Focus to Become a Highly Productive (and Peaceful!) Person

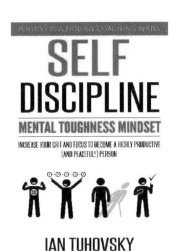

This Mindset and Exercises Will Help You Build Everlasting Self-Discipline and Unbeatable Willpower

Imagine that you have this rare kind of power that enables you to maintain iron resolve, crystal clarity, and everyday focus to gradually realize all of your dreams by consistently ticking one goal after another off your to-do list.

Way too often, people and their minds don't really play in one team.

Wouldn't that be profoundly life-changing to utilize that power to make the best partners with your brain?

This rare kind of power is a mindset. The way you think, the way you perceive and handle both the world around you and your inner reality, will ultimately determine the quality of your life.

A single shift in your perception can trigger meaningful results.

Life can be tough. Whenever we turn, there are obstacles blocking our way. Some are caused by our environment, and some by ourselves. Yet, we all know people who are able to overcome them consistently, and, simply speaking, become successful. And stay there!

What really elevates a regular Joe or Jane to superhero status is the laser-sharp focus, perseverance, and the ability to keep on going when everyone else would have quit.
I have, for a long time, studied the lives of the most disciplined people on this planet. In this book, you are going to learn their secrets.
No matter if your goals are financial, sport, relationship, or habit-changing oriented, this book covers it all.

Today, I want to share with you the science-based insights and field-tested methods that have helped me, my friends, and my clients change their lives and become real-life go-getters.

Here are some of the things you will learn from this book:

- **What the "positive thinking trap" means,** and how exactly should you use the power of positivity to actually help yourself instead of holding yourself back?
- What truly makes us happy and how does that relate to success? Is it money? Social position? Friends, family? Health? **No. There's actually something bigger, deeper, and much more fundamental behind our happiness.** You will be surprised to find out what the factor that ultimately drives us and keeps us going is, and this discovery can greatly improve your life.
- **Why our Western perception of both happiness and success are fundamentally wrong**, and how those misperceptions can kill your chances of succeeding?
- **Why relying on willpower and motivation is a very bad idea, and what to hold on to instead?** This is as important as using only the best gasoline in a top-grade sports car. Fill its engine with a moped fuel and keep the engine oil level low, and it won't get far. Your mind is this sports car engine. I will show you where to get this quality fuel from.
- **You will learn what the common denominator of the most successful and disciplined people on this planet is** – Navy SEALS and other special forces, Shaolin monks, top performing CEOs and Athletes, they, in fact, have a lot in common. I studied their lives for a long time, and now, it's time to share this knowledge with you.
- Why your entire life can be viewed as a piece of training, and **what are the rules of this training?**
- What the XX-th century Russian Nobel-Prize winner and long-forgotten genius Japanese psychotherapist **can teach you about the importance of your emotions and utilizing them correctly in your quest to becoming a self-disciplined and a peaceful person?**
- How modern science can help you **overcome temptation and empower your will**, and why following strict and inconvenient diets or regimens can actually help you achieve your goals in the end?
- How can you win by failing and **why giving up on some of your goals can actually be a good thing?**
- How do we often become **our own biggest enemies** in achieving our goals and how to finally change it?
- How to **maintain** your success once you achieve it?

Direct Buy Link to Amazon Kindle Store:
http://tinyurl.com/IanMentalToughness
Paperback version on Createspace: http://tinyurl.com/IanMTPaperback

Confidence: Your Practical Training: How to Develop Healthy Self Esteem and Deep Self Confidence to Be Successful and Become True Friends with Yourself

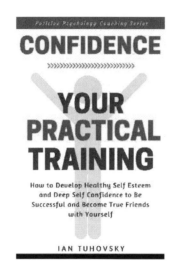

Have you ever considered how many opportunities you have missed and how many chances you have wasted by lacking self-confidence when you need it most?

Have you ever given up on your plans, important goals, and dreams not because you just decided to focus on something else, but simply because you were too SCARED or hesitant to even start, or stick up to the plan and keep going?

Are you afraid of starting your own business or asking for a promotion? Petrified of public speaking, socializing, dating, taking up new hobbies, or going to job interviews?

Can you imagine how amazing and relieving it would feel to finally obtain all the self-esteem needed to accomplish things you've always wanted to achieve in your life?

Finally, have you ever found yourself in a situation where you simply couldn't understand **WHY you acted in a certain way**, or why you kept holding yourself back and feeling all the bad emotions, instead of just going for what's the most important to you?

Due to early social conditioning and many other influences, most people on this planet are already familiar with all these feelings.

WAY TOO FAMILIAR!

I know how it feels, too. I was in the same exact place.

And then, I found the way!
It's high time you did something about it too because, truth be told, self-confident people just have it way easier in every single aspect of life!

From becoming your own boss or succeeding in your career, through dating and socializing, to starting new hobbies, standing up for yourself or maybe finally packing your suitcase and going on this Asia trip you promised yourself decades ago... All too often, people fail in these quests as they aren't equipped with the natural and lasting self-confidence to deal with them in a proper way.

Confidence is not useful only in everyday life and casual situations. Do you really want to fulfill your wildest dreams, or do you just want to keep chatting about them with your friends, until one day you wake up as a grumpy, old, frustrated person?
Big achievements require brave and fearless actions. If you want to act bravely, you need to be confident.

Along with lots of useful, practical exercises, this book will provide you with plenty of new information that will help you understand what confidence problems really come down to. And this is the most important and the saddest part, because most people do not truly recognize the root problem, and that's why they get poor results.

Lack of self-confidence and problems with unhealthy self-esteem are usually the reason why smart, competent, and talented people never achieve a satisfying life; a life that should easily be possible for them.

In this book, you will read about:
-How, when, and why society robs us all of natural confidence and healthy self-esteem.
-What kind of social and psychological traps you need to avoid in order to feel much calmer, happier, and more confident.
-What "natural confidence" means and how it becomes natural.
-What "self-confidence" really is and what it definitely isn't (as opposed to what most people think!).
-How your mind hurts you when it really just wants to help you, and how to stop the process.
-What different kinds of fear we feel, where they come from, and how to defeat them.
-How to have a great relationship with yourself.
-How to use stress to boost your inner strength.
-Effective and ineffective ways of building healthy self-esteem.
-Why the relation between self-acceptance and stress is so crucial.
-How to stay confident in professional situations.
-How to protect your self-esteem when life brings you down, and how to deal with criticism and jealousy.
-How to use neuro-linguistic programming, imagination, visualizations, diary entries, and your five senses to re-program your subconscious and get rid of "mental viruses" and detrimental beliefs that actively destroy your natural confidence and healthy self-esteem.
Take the right action and start changing your life for the better today!

DOWNLOAD FOR FREE from Amazon Kindle Store:

https://tinyurl.com/IanConfidenceTraining
Paperback version on Createspace:
http://tinyurl.com/IanConfidencePaperbackV

Mindfulness: The Most Effective Techniques: Connect With Your Inner Self to Reach Your Goals Easily and Peacefully

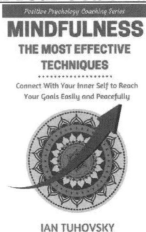

Mindfulness is not about complicated and otherworldly woo-woo spiritual practices. It doesn't require you to be a part of any religion or a movement.

What mindfulness is about is living a good life (that's quite practical, right?), and this book is all about deepening your awareness, **getting to know yourself**, and developing attitudes and mental habits that will make you not only a successful and effective person in life, but a happy and wise one as well.

If you have ever wondered what the mysterious words "mindfulness" means and why would anyone bother, you have just found your (detailed) answer!

This book will provide you with actionable steps and valuable information, all in plain English, so all of your doubts will be soon gone.

In my experience, **nothing has proven as simple and yet effective and powerful as the daily practice of mindfulness.**

It has helped me become more decisive, disciplined, focused, calm, and just a happier person.

I can come as far as to say that mindfulness has transformed me into a success.

Now, it's your turn.
There's nothing to lose, and so much to win!

The payoff is nothing less than transforming your life into its true potential.

What you will learn from this book:

-What exactly does the word "mindfulness" mean, and why should it become an important word in your dictionary?

-How taking **as little as five minutes a day** to clear your mind might result in steering your life towards great success and becoming a much more fulfilled person? ...and **how the heck can you "clear your mind" exactly?**

-What are the **most interesting, effective, and not well-known mindfulness techniques for success** that I personally use to stay on the track and achieve my goals daily while feeling calm and relaxed?

-**Where to start** and how to slowly get into mindfulness to avoid unnecessary confusion?

-What are the **scientifically proven profits** of a daily mindfulness practice?

-**How to develop the so-called "Nonjudgmental Awareness"** to win with discouragement and negative thoughts, **stick to the practice** and keep becoming a more focused, calm, disciplined, and peaceful person on a daily basis?

-What are **the most common problems** experienced by practitioners of mindfulness and meditation, and how to overcome them?

-How to meditate and **just how easy** can it be?

-What are **the most common mistakes** people keep doing when trying to get into meditation and mindfulness? How to avoid them?

-**Real life tested steps** to apply mindfulness to everyday life to become happier and much more successful person?

-What is the relation between mindfulness and life success? How to use mindfulness to become much more effective in your life and achieve your goals much easier?

-**What to do in life** when just about everything seems to go wrong?

-How to become a **more patient and disciplined person**?

Stop existing and start living.
Start changing your life for the better today.

DOWNLOAD FOR FREE from Amazon Kindle Store:

myBook.to/IanMindfulnessGuide
Paperback version on Createspace:

http://tinyurl.com/IanMindfulnessGuide

Meditation for Beginners: How to Meditate (as an Ordinary Person!)

to Relieve Stress and Be Successful

Meditation doesn't have to be about crystals, hypnotic folk music and incense sticks! **Forget about sitting in unnatural and uncomfortable positions while going, "Ommmmm...."** It is not necessarily a club full of yoga masters, Shaolin monks, hippies and new-agers.

It is a super useful and universal practice which can improve your overall brain performance and happiness. When meditating, you take a step back from actively thinking your thoughts, and instead see them for what they are. The reason why meditation is helpful in reducing stress and attaining peace is that it gives your over-active consciousness a break.

Just like your body needs it, your mind does too!

I give you the gift of peace that I was able to attain through present moment awareness.

Direct Buy Link to Amazon Kindle Store:

https://tinyurl.com/IanMeditationGuide

Paperback version on Createspace: http://tinyurl.com/ianmeditationpaperback

Zen: Beginner's Guide: Happy, Peaceful and Focused Lifestyle for Everyone

Contrary to popular belief, Zen is not a discipline reserved for monks practicing Kung Fu. Although there is some truth to this idea, Zen is a practice that is applicable, useful and pragmatic for anyone to study regardless of what religion you follow (or don't follow).

Zen is the practice of studying your subconscious and **seeing your true nature.** The purpose of this work is to show you how to apply and utilize the teachings and essence of Zen in everyday life in the Western society. I'm not really an "absolute truth seeker" unworldly type of person—I just believe in practical plans and blueprints that actually help in living a better life. Of course I will tell you about the origin of Zen and the traditional ways of practicing it, but I will also show you my side of things, my personal point of view and translation of many Zen truths into a more "contemporary" and practical language.

It is a "modern Zen lifestyle" type of book.

What You Will Read About:
- Where Did Zen Come from? - A short history and explanation of Zen
- What Does Zen Teach? - The major teachings and precepts of Zen
- Various Zen meditation techniques that are applicable and practical for everyone!
- The Benefits of a Zen Lifestyle
- What Zen Buddhism is NOT?
- How to Slow Down and Start Enjoying Your Life
- How to Accept Everything and Lose Nothing
- Why Being Alone Can Be Beneficial
- Why Pleasure Is NOT Happiness
- Six Ways to Practically Let Go
- How to De-clutter Your Life and Live Simply
- "Mindfulness on Steroids"
- How to Take Care of Your Awareness and Focus
- Where to Start and How to Practice Zen as a Regular Person
- And many other interesting concepts...

I invite you to take this journey into the peaceful world of Zen Buddhism with me today!
Direct Buy Link to Amazon Kindle Store: https://tinyurl.com/IanZenGuide

Paperback version on Createspace: http://tinyurl.com/IanZenPaperbackV

Buddhism: Beginner's Guide: Bring Peace and Happiness to Your Everyday Life

Buddhism is one of the most practical and simple belief systems on this planet, and it has greatly helped me on my way to become a better person in every aspect possible. In this book I will show you what happened and how it was.

No matter if you are totally green when it comes to Buddha's teachings or maybe you have already heard something about them—this book will help you systematize your knowledge and will inspire you to learn more and to take steps to make your life positively better!

I invite you to take this beautiful journey into the graceful and meaningful world of Buddhism with me today!

Direct link to Amazon Kindle Store: https://tinyurl.com/IanBuddhismGuide
Paperback version on Createspace: http://tinyurl.com/ianbuddhismpaperback

About The Author

Author's Blog: www.mindfulnessforsuccess.com
Amazon Author Page: http://www.amazon.com/author/iantuhovsky/

Hi! I'm Ian...

. . . and I am interested in life. I am in the study of having an awesome and passionate life, which I believe is within the reach of practically everyone. I'm not a mentor or a guru. I'm just a guy who always knew there was more than we are told. I managed to turn my life around from way below my expectations to a really satisfying one, and now I want to share this fascinating journey with you so that you can do it, too.

I was born and raised somewhere in Eastern Europe, where Polar Bears eat people on the streets, we munch on snow instead of ice cream and there's only vodka instead of tap water, but since I make a living out of several different businesses, I move to a new country every couple of months. I also work as an HR consultant for various European companies.

I love self-development, traveling, recording music and providing value by helping others. I passionately read and write about social psychology, sociology, NLP, meditation, mindfulness, eastern philosophy, emotional intelligence, time management, communication skills and all of the topics related to conscious self-development and being the most awesome version of yourself.

Breathe. Relax. Feel that you're alive and smile. And never hesitate to contact me!

Printed in Great Britain
by Amazon